A STUDY
OF
RELIGION

SWAMI VIVEKANANDA

Advaita Ashrama
(Publication Department)
5 DEHI ENTALLY ROAD
CALCUTTA 700 014

Published by
Swami Mumukshananda
President, Advaita Ashrama
Mayavati, Champawat, Himalayas, U.P.
from its Publication Department, Calcutta

Twelfth Impression, September 1998
3M3C

ISBN 81-7505-036-5

Printed in India at
Gipidi Box Company
3B Chatu Babu Lane
Calcutta 700 014

PUBLISHER'S NOTE
TO THE ELEVENTH EDITION

The first ten editions of this book were published by Udbodhan Office, Calcutta. The copyright of the book having been recently made over to us, we deem it a privilege to bring out this new edition. The text has been compared with the original lectures as they occur in the *Complete Works of Swami Vivekananda*.

Swami Vivekananda's illuminative ideas on religion are spread over nearly 4200 pages of his Complete Works. The present compilation of eight lectures out of them serves as a small introduction to his voluminous writings, talks, and lectures on the subject.

We hope this collection will immensely help the readers grasp the phenomenon of religion in a broad and rational perspective and lead them to read other lectures and writings of Swamiji for further knowledge, information, and inspiration.

5 April 1995   PUBLISHER

PUBLISHER'S NOTE
TO THE ELEVENTH EDITION

The first ten editions of this book were published by Udbodhan Office, Calcutta. The copyright of the book having been recently made over to us, we deem it a privilege to bring out this new edition. The text has been compared with the original lectures as they occur in the Complete Works of Swami Vivekananda.

Swami Vivekananda's illuminative ideas on religion are spread over nearly 4200 pages of his Complete Works. The present compilation of eight lectures out of them serves as a small introduction to his voluminous writings, talks, and lectures on the subject.

We hope this collection will immensely help the readers grasp the phenomenon of religion in a broad and rational perspective and lead them to read other lectures and writings of Swamiji for further knowledge, information, and inspiration.

5 April 1993   PUBLISHER

CONTENTS

WHAT IS RELIGION?

(Class Lecture at Vedanta Society of New York on June 17, 1900)

A huge locomotive has rushed on over the line and a small worm that was creeping upon one of the rails saved its life by crawling out of the path of the locomotive. Yet this little worm, so insignificant that it can be crushed in a moment, is a living something, while this locomotive, so huge, so immense, is only an engine, a machine. You say the one has life and the other is only dead matter and all its powers and strength and speed are only those of a dead machine, a mechanical contrivance. Yet the poor little worm which moved upon the rail and which the least touch of the engine would have deprived of its life is a majestic being compared to that huge locomotive. It is a small part of the Infinite and, therefore, it is greater than this powerful engine. Why should that be so? How do we know the living from the dead? The machine mechanically performs all the movements its maker made it to perform, its movements are not those of life. How can we make the distinction between the living and the dead, then? In the living there is freedom, there is intelligence; in the dead all is bound and no freedom is possible, because there is no intelligence. This freedom that distinguishes us from mere machines is what we are all striving for. To be more free is the goal of all our efforts, for only in perfect freedom can there be perfection. This effort to attain freedom underlies all forms of worship, whether we know it or not.

If we were to examine the various sorts of worship all over the world, we would see that the rudest of mankind are worshipping ghosts, demons, and the spirits of their forefathers—serpent worship, worship of tribal gods, and worship of the departed ones. Why do they do this? Because they feel that in some unknown way these beings are greater, more powerful than themselves, and limit their freedom. They, therefore, seek to propitiate these beings in order to prevent them from molesting them, in other words, to get more freedom. They also seek to win favour from these superior beings, to get by gift of the gods what ought to be earned by personal effort.

On the whole, this shows that the world is expecting a miracle. This expectation never leaves us, and however we may try, we are all running after the miraculous and extraordinary. What is mind but that ceaseless inquiry into the meaning and mystery of life? We may say that only uncultivated people are going after all these things, but the question still is there: Why should it be so? The Jews were asking for a miracle. The whole world has been asking for the same these thousands of years. There is, again, the universal dissatisfaction. We make an ideal but we have rushed only half the way after it when we make a newer one. We struggle hard to attain to some goal and then discover we do not want it. This dissatisfaction we are having time after time, and what is there in the mind if there is to be only dissatisfaction? What is the meaning of this universal dissatisfaction? It is because freedom is every man's goal. He seeks it ever, his whole life is a struggle after it. The child rebels against law as soon as it is born. Its first utterance is a cry, a protest against the bondage in which it finds itself. This longing for freedom produces the idea of a Being who is absolutely free. The concept of God is a fundamental element in the human constitution. In the Vedanta, Sat-chit-ānanda (Existence-Knowledge-Bliss) is the highest concept of God possible to the mind. It is the essence of knowledge and is by its nature the essence of bliss. We have been stifling that inner voice long enough, seeking to follow law and quiet the human nature, but there is that human instinct to rebel against nature's laws. We may not understand what the meaning is, but there is that unconscious struggle of the human with the spiritual, of the lower with the higher mind, and the struggle attempts to preserve one's separate life, what we call our 'individuality'.

Even hells stand out with this miraculous fact that we are born rebels; and the first fact of life—the inrushing of life itself—against this we rebel and cry out, 'No law for us.' As long as we obey the laws we are like machines, and on goes the universe, and we cannot break it. Laws as laws become man's nature. The first inkling of life on its higher level is in seeing this struggle within us to break the bond of nature and to be free. 'Freedom, O Freedom! Freedom, O Freedom!' is the song of the soul. Bondage, alas, to be bound in nature, seems its fate.

Why should there be serpent, or ghost, or demon worship and all these various creeds and forms for having miracles? Why do we say that there is life, there is being in anything? There must be a meaning in all this search, this endeavour to understand life, to explain being. It is not meaningless and vain. It is man's ceaseless endeavour to become free. The knowledge which we now call science has been struggling for thousands of years in its attempt to gain freedom, and people ask for freedom. Yet there is no freedom in nature. It is all law. Still the struggle goes on. Nay, the whole of nature from the very sun to the atoms is under law, and even for man there is no freedom. But we cannot believe it. We have been studying laws from the beginning and yet cannot—nay, will not—believe that man is under law. The soul cries ever, 'Freedom, O Freedom!' With the conception of God as a perfectly free Being, man cannot rest eternally in this bondage. Higher he must go, and unless the struggle were for himself, he would think it too severe. Man says to himself, 'I am a born slave, I am bound; nevertheless, there is a Being who is not bound by nature. He is free and Master of nature.'

The conception of God, therefore, is as essential and

as fundamental a part of mind as is the idea of bondage. Both are the outcome of the idea of freedom. There cannot be life, even in the plant, without the idea of freedom. In the plant or in the worm, life has to rise to the individual concept. It is there, unconsciously working, the plant living its life to preserve the variety, principle, or form, not nature. The idea of nature controlling every step onward overrules the idea of freedom. Onward goes the idea of the material world, onward moves the idea of freedom. Still the fight goes on. We are hearing about all the quarrels of creeds and sects, yet creeds and sects are just and proper, they must be there. The chain is lengthening and naturally the struggle increases, but there need be no quarrels if we only knew that we are all striving to reach the same goal.

The embodiment of freedom, the Master of nature, is what we call God. You cannot deny Him. No, because you cannot move or live without the idea of freedom. Would you come here if you did not believe you were free? It is quite possible that the biologist can and will give some explanation of this perpetual effort to be free. Take all that for granted, still the idea of freedom is there. It is a fact, as much so as the other fact that you cannot apparently get over, the fact of being under nature.

Bondage and liberty, light and shadow, good and evil must be there, but the very fact of the bondage shows also this freedom hidden there. If one is a fact, the other is equally a fact. There must be this idea of freedom. While now we cannot see that this idea of bondage, in uncultivated man, is his struggle for freedom, yet the idea of freedom is there. The bondage of sin and impurity in the uncultivated savage is to his consciousness very small, for his nature is only a little higher than the animal's. What he struggles against is the bondage of physical nature, the lack of physical gratification, but out of this lower consciousness grows and broadens the higher conception of a mental or moral bondage and a longing for spiritual freedom. Here we see the divine dimly shining through the veil of ignorance. The veil is very dense at first and the light may be almost obscured, but it is there, ever pure and undimmed—the radiant fire of freedom and perfection. Man personifies this as the Ruler of the Universe, the One Free Being. He does not yet know that the universe is all one, that the difference is only in degree, in the concept.

The whole of nature is worship of God. Wherever there is life, there is this search for freedom and that freedom is the same as God. Necessarily this freedom gives us mastery over all nature and is impossible without knowledge. The more we are knowing, the more we are becoming masters of nature. Mastery alone is making us strong and if there be some being entirely free and master of nature, that being must have a perfect knowledge of nature, must be omnipresent and omniscient. Freedom must go hand in hand with these, and that being alone who has acquired these will be beyond nature.

Blessedness, eternal peace, arising from perfect freedom, is the highest concept of religion underlying all the ideas of God in Vedanta—absolutely free Existence, not bound by anything, no change, no nature, nothing that

can produce a change in Him. This same freedom is in you
and in me and is the only real freedom.

God is still, established upon His own majestic
changeless Self. You and I try to be one with Him, but
plant ourselves upon nature, upon the trifles of daily life,
on money, on fame, on human love, and all these changing
forms in nature which make for bondage. When nature
shines, upon what depends the shining? Upon God and
not upon the sun, nor the moon, nor the stars. Wherever
anything shines, whether it is the light in the sun or in our
own consciousness, it is He. He shining, all shines after
Him.

Now we have seen that this God is self-evident,
impersonal, omniscient, the Knower and Master of nature,
the Lord of all. He is behind all worship and it is being
done according to Him, whether we know it or not. I go
one step further. That at which all marvel, that which we
call evil, is His worship too. This too is a part of freedom.
Nay, I will be terrible even and tell you that, when you are
doing evil, the impulse behind is also that freedom. It may
have been misguided and misled, but it was there; and
there cannot be any life or any impulse unless that
freedom be behind it. Freedom breathes in the throb of the
universe. Unless there is unity at the universal heart we
cannot understand variety. Such is the conception of the
Lord in the Upanishads. Sometimes it rises even higher,
presenting to us an ideal before which at first we
stand aghast—that we are in essence one with God. He
who is the colouring in the wings of the butterfly, and the

blossoming of the rose-bud, is the power that is in the plant and in the butterfly. He who gives us life is the power within us. Out of His fire comes life, and the direst death is also His power. He whose shadow is death, His shadow is immortality also. Take a still higher conception. See how we are flying like hunted hares from all that is terrible, and like them, hiding our heads and thinking we are safe. See how the whole world is flying from everything terrible. Once when I was in Varanasi, I was passing through a place where there was a large tank of water on one side and a high wall on the other. It was in the grounds where there were many monkeys. The monkeys of Varanasi are huge brutes and are sometimes surly. They now took it into their heads not to allow me to pass through their street, so they howled and shrieked and clutched at my feet as I passed. As they pressed closer, I began to run, but the faster I ran, the faster came the monkeys and they began to bite at me. It seemed impossible to escape, but just then I met a stranger who called out to me, 'Face the brutes.' I turned and faced the monkeys, and they fell back and finally fled. That is a lesson for all life—face the terrible, face it boldly. Like the monkeys, the hardships of life fall back when we cease to flee before them. If we are ever to gain freedom, it must be by conquering nature, never by running away. Cowards never win victories. We have to fight fear and troubles and ignorance if we expect them to flee before us.

What is death? What are terrors? Do you not see the Lord's face in them? Fly from evil and terror and misery, and they will follow you. Face them, and they will flee. The whole world worships ease and pleasure, and very few dare to worship that which is painful. To rise above both is the idea of freedom. Unless man passes through this gate he cannot be free. We all have to face these. We strive to worship the Lord, but the body rises between, nature rises between Him and us and blinds our vision. We must learn how to worship and love Him in the thunderbolt, in shame, in sorrow, in sin. All the world has ever been preaching the God of virtue. I preach a God of virtue and a God of sin in one. Take Him if you dare—that is the one way to salvation; then alone will come to us the Truth Ultimate which comes from the idea of oneness. Then will be lost the idea that one is greater than another. The nearer we approach the law of freedom, the more we shall come under the Lord, and troubles will vanish. Then we shall not differentiate the door of hell from the gate of heaven, nor differentiate between men and say, 'I am greater than any being in the universe.' Until we see nothing in the world but the Lord Himself, all these evils will beset us and we shall make all these distinctions; because it is only in the Lord, in the Spirit, that we are all one; and until we see God everywhere, this unity will not exist for us.

Two birds of beautiful plumage, inseparable companions, sat upon the same tree, one on the top and one below. The beautiful bird below was eating the fruits of the tree, sweet and bitter, one moment a sweet one and another a bitter. The moment he ate a bitter fruit, he was sorry, but after a while he ate another and when it too was bitter, he looked up and saw the other bird who ate neither the sweet nor the bitter, but was calm and majestic, immersed in his own glory. And then the poor lower bird forgot and went on eating the sweet and bitter fruits again, until at last he ate one that was extremely bitter; and then he stopped again and once more looked up at the glorious bird above. Then he came nearer and nearer to the other bird; and when he had come near enough, rays of light shone upon him, and enveloped him, and he saw he was transformed into the higher bird. He became calm, majestic, free, and found that there had been but one bird all the time on the tree. The lower bird was but the reflection of the one above. So we are in reality one with the Lord, but the reflection makes us seem many, as when the one sun reflects in a million dewdrops and seems a million tiny suns. The reflection must vanish if we are to identify ourselves with our real nature which is divine. The universe itself can never be the limit of our satisfaction. That is why the miser gathers more and more money, that is why the robber robs, the sinner sins, that is why you are learning philosophy. All have one purpose. There is no other purpose in life, save to reach this freedom. Consciously or unconsciously, we are all striving for perfection. Every being must attain to it.

The man who is groping through sin, through misery, the man who is choosing the path through hells, will reach it, but it will take time. We cannot save him. Some hard knocks on his head will help him to turn to the Lord. The path of virtue, purity, unselfishness, spirituality, becomes known at last and what all are doing unconsciously, we are trying to do consciously. The idea is expressed by St. Paul, 'The God that ye ignorantly worship, Him declare I unto you.' This is the lesson for the whole world to learn. What have these philosophies and theories of nature to do, if not to help us to attain to this one goal in life? Let us come to that consciousness of the identity of everything and let man see himself in everything. Let us be no more the worshippers of creeds or sects with small limited notions of God, but see Him in everything in the universe. If you are knowers of God, you will everywhere find the same worship as in your own heart.

Get rid, in the first place, of all these limited ideas and see God in every person—working through all hands, walking through all feet, and eating through every mouth. In every being He lives, through all minds He thinks. He is self-evident, nearer unto us than ourselves. To know this is religion, is faith, and may it please the Lord to give us this faith! When we shall feel that oneness, we shall be immortal. We are physically immortal even, one with the universe. So long as there is one that breathes throughout the universe, I live in that one. I am not this limited little being, I am the universal. I am the life of all the sons of the past. I am the soul of Buddha, of Jesus, of Mohammed. I am the soul of all the teachers, and I am all the robbers that robbed, and all the murderers that were hanged, I am the universal. Stand up then; this is the highest worship. You are one with the universe. That only is humility—not

crawling upon all fours and calling yourself a sinner. That
is the highest evolution when this veil of differentiation is
torn off. The highest creed is Oneness. I am so-and-so is a
limited idea, not true of the real 'I'. I am the universal;
stand upon that and ever worship the Highest through the
highest form, for God is Spirit and should be worshipped
in spirit and in truth. Through lower forms of worship,
man's material thoughts rise to spiritual worship and the
Universal Infinite One is at last worshipped in and
through the spirit. That which is limited is material. The
Spirit alone is infinite. God is spirit, is infinite; man is spirit
and, therefore, infinite, and the Infinite alone can worship
the Infinite. We will worship the Infinite; that is the
highest spiritual worship. The grandeur of realising these
ideas, how difficult it is! I theorise, talk, philosophise; and
the next moment something comes against me, and I unconsciously become angry, I forget there is anything in the
universe but this little limited self, I forget to say, 'I am the
Spirit, what is this trifle to me? I am the Spirit.' I forget it is
all myself playing, I forget God, I forget freedom.

Sharp as the blade of a razor, long and difficult and
hard to cross, is the way to freedom. The sages have
declared this again and again. Yet do not let these weak-
nesses and failures bind you. The Upanishads have
declared: 'Arise! Awake! and stop not until the goal is
reached.' We will then certainly cross the path, sharp as it
is like the razor, and long and distant and difficult though
it be. Man becomes the master of gods and demons. No
one is to blame for our miseries but ourselves. Do you

think there is only a dark cup of poison if man goes to look for nectar? The nectar is there and is for every man who strives to reach it. The Lord Himself tells us, 'Give up all these paths and struggles. Do thou take refuge in Me. I will take thee to the other shore, be not afraid.' We hear that from all the scriptures of the world that come to us. The same voice teaches us to say, 'Thy will be done upon earth, as it is in heaven,' for 'Thine is the kingdom and the power and the glory.' It is difficult, all very difficult. I say to myself, 'This moment I will take refuge in Thee, O Lord. Unto Thy love I will sacrifice all, and on Thine altar I will place all that is good and virtuous. My sins, my sorrows, my actions, good and evil, I will offer unto Thee; do Thou take them and I will never forget.' One moment I say, 'Thy will be done,' and the next moment something comes to try me and I spring up in a rage. The goal of all religions is the same but the language of the teachers differs. The attempt is to kill the false 'I', so that the real 'I', the Lord, will reign. 'I the Lord thy God am a jealous God. Thou shalt have no other gods before me,' say the Hebrew scriptures. God must be there all alone. We must say, 'Not I, but Thou,' and then we should give up everything but the Lord. He, and He alone, should reign. Perhaps we struggle hard and yet the next moment our feet slip, and then we try to stretch out our hands to Mother. We find we cannot stand alone. Life is infinite, one chapter of which is, 'Thy will be done,' and unless we realise all the chapters we cannot realise the whole. 'Thy will be done'—every moment the traitor mind rebels against it, yet it must be said, again and again, if we are to conquer the lower self. We cannot serve a traitor and yet be saved. There is salvation for all except the traitor and we stand condemned as traitors, traitors against our own selves, against the majesty of Mother, when we refuse to obey the voice of our higher Self. Come what will, we must give our bodies and minds up to the Supreme Will. Well has it been said by the Hindu philosopher, 'If man says twice, "Thy will be done," he commits sin.' 'Thy will be done,' what more is needed, why say it twice? What is good is good. No more shall we take it back. 'Thy will be done on earth as it is in heaven, for Thine is the kingdom and the power and the glory for evermore.'

(*Complete Works of Swami Vivekananda*,
1992, vol. 1, pp. 333–43.)

THE NECESSITY OF RELIGION

(Delivered at London Royal Institute of Painters in Watercolours on June 7, 1896)

Of all the forces that have worked and are still working to mould the destinies of the human race, none, certainly, is more potent than that, the manifestation of which we call religion. All social organisations have as a background, somewhere, the workings of that peculiar force, and the greatest cohesive impulse ever brought into play amongst human units has been derived from this power. It is obvious to all of us that in very many cases the bonds of religion have proved stronger than the bonds of race, or climate, or even of descent. It is a well-known fact that persons worshipping the same God, believing in the same religion, have stood by each other, with much greater strength and constancy, than people of merely the same descent, or even brothers. Various attempts have been made to trace the beginnings of religion. In all the ancient religions which have come down to us at the present day, we find one claim made—that they are all supernatural, that their genesis is not, as it were, in the human brain, but that they have originated somewhere outside of it.

Two theories have gained some acceptance amongst modern scholars. One is the spirit theory of religion, the other the evolution of the idea of the Infinite. One party maintains that ancestor worship is the beginning of religious ideas; the other, that religion originates in the personification of the powers of nature. Man wants to keep up the memory of his dead relatives, and thinks they are living even when the body is dissolved, and he wants to place food for them and, in a certain sense, to worship them. Out of that came the growth we call religion.

Studying the ancient religions of the Egyptians, Babylonians, Chinese, and many other races in America and elsewhere, we find very clear traces of this ancestor worship being the beginning of religion. With the ancient Egyptians, the first idea of the soul was that of a double. Every human body contained in it another being very similar to it; and when a man died, this double went out of the body and yet lived on. But the life of the double lasted only so long as the dead body remained intact, and that is why we find among the Egyptians so much solicitude to keep the body uninjured. And that is why they built those huge pyramids in which they preserved the bodies. For, if any portion of the external body was hurt, the double would be correspondingly injured. This is clearly ancestor worship. With the ancient Babylonians we find the same idea of the double, but with a variation. The double lost all sense of love; it frightened the living to give it food and drink, and to help it in various ways. It even lost all affection for its own children and its own wife. Among the ancient Hindus also, we find traces of this ancestor worship. Among the Chinese, the basis of their religion may also be said to be ancestor worship, and it still permeates the length and breadth of that vast country. In fact, the only religion that can really be said to flourish in China is that of ancestor worship. Thus it seems, on the one hand, a very good position is made out for those who hold the theory of ancestor worship as the beginning of religion.

On the other hand, there are scholars who from the ancient Aryan literature show that religion originated in nature worship. Although in India we find proofs of ancestor worship everywhere, yet in the oldest records there is no trace of it whatsoever. In the Rig-Veda Samhita, the most ancient record of the Aryan race, we do not find any trace of it. Modern scholars think it is the worship of nature that they find there. The human mind seems to struggle to get a peep behind the scenes. The dawn, the evening, the hurricane, the stupendous and gigantic forces of nature, its beauties, these have exercised the human mind, and it aspires to go beyond, to understand something about them. In the struggle they endow these phenomena with personal attributes, giving them souls and bodies, sometimes beautiful, sometimes transcendent.

Every attempt ends by these phenomena becoming abstractions whether personalised or not. So also it is found with the ancient Greeks; their whole mythology is simply this abstracted nature worship. So also with the ancient Germans, the Scandinavians, and all the other Aryan races. Thus, on this side too, a very strong case has been made out, that religion has its origin in the personification of the powers of nature.

These two views, though they seem to be contradictory, can be reconciled on a third basis, which, to my mind, is the real germ of religion, and that I propose to call the struggle to transcend the limitations of the senses. Either, man goes to seek for the spirits of his ancestors, the spirits of the dead, that is, he wants to get a glimpse of what there is after the body is dissolved, or, he desires to understand the power working behind the stupendous phenomena of nature. Whichever of these is the case, one thing is certain, that he tries to transcend the limitations of the senses. He cannot remain satisfied with his senses; he wants to go beyond them. The explanation need not be mysterious. To me it seems very natural that the first glimpse of religion should come through dreams. The first idea of immortality man may well get through dreams. Is that not a most wonderful state? And we know that children and untutored minds find very little difference between dreaming and their awakened state. What can be more natural than that they find, as natural logic, that even during the sleep state, when the body is apparently dead, the mind goes on with all its intricate workings? What wonder that men will at once come to the conclusion that when this body is dissolved for ever, the same working will go on? This, to my mind, would be a more natural explanation of the supernatural, and through this dream idea the human mind rises to higher and higher conceptions. Of course, in time, the vast majority of mankind found out that these dreams are not verified by their waking states, and that during the dream state it is not that man has a fresh existence, but simply that he recapitulates the experiences of the awakened state.

But by this time the search had begun, and the search was inward, and man continued inquiring more deeply into the different stages of the mind and discovered higher states than either the waking or the dreaming. This state of things we find in all the organised religions of the world, called either ecstasy or inspiration. In all organised religions, their founders, prophets, and messengers are declared to have gone into states of mind that were neither waking nor sleeping, in which they came face to face with a new series of facts relating to what is called the spiritual kingdom. They realised things there much more intensely than we realise facts around us in our waking state. Take, for instance, the religions of the Brahmins. The Vedas are said to have been written by Rishis. These Rishis were sages who realised certain facts. The exact definition of the Sanskrit word Rishi is a Seer of Mantras—of the thoughts conveyed in the Vedic hymns. These men declared that they had realised—sensed, if that word can be used with regard to the supersensuous—certain facts, and these facts they proceeded to put on record. We find the same truth declared amongst both the Jews and the Christians.

Some exceptions may be taken in the case of the Buddhists as represented by the Southern sect. It may be asked—if the Buddhists do not believe in any God or soul, how can their religion be derived from the supersensuous state of existence? The answer to this is that even the Buddhists find an eternal moral law, and that moral law was not reasoned out in our sense of the word. But Buddha found it, discovered it, in a supersensuous state. Those of you who have studied the life of Buddha, even as briefly given in that beautiful poem, *The Light of Asia*, may remember that Buddha is represented as sitting under the Bo-tree until he reached that supersensuous state of mind. All his teachings came through this, and not through intellectual cogitations.

Thus a tremendous statement is made by all religions; that the human mind, at certain moments, transcends not only the limitations of the senses, but also the power of reasoning. It then comes face to face with facts which it could never have sensed, could never have reasoned out. These facts are the basis of all the religions of the world. Of course we have the right to challenge these facts, to put them to the test of reason. Nevertheless, all the existing religions of the world claim for the human mind this peculiar power of transcending the limits of the senses and the limits of reason; and this power they put forward as a statement of fact.

Apart from the consideration of the question how far

these facts claimed by religions are true, we find one characteristic common to them all. They are all abstractions as contrasted with the concrete discoveries of physics, for instance; and in all the highly organised religions they take the purest form of Unit Abstraction, either in the form of an Abstracted Presence, as an Omnipresent Being, as an Abstract Personality called God, as a Moral Law, or in the form of an Abstract Essence underlying every existence. In modern times, too, the attempts made to preach religions without appealing to the supersensuous state of the mind have had to take up the old abstractions of the Ancients and give different names to them, as 'Moral Law,' the 'Ideal Unity,' and so forth, thus showing that these abstractions are not in the senses. None of us have yet seen an 'Ideal Human Being', and yet we are told to believe in it. None of us have yet seen an ideally perfect man, and yet without that ideal we cannot progress. Thus, this one fact stands out from all these different religions, that there is an Ideal Unit Abstraction, which is put before us, either in the form of a Person or an Impersonal Being, or a Law, or a Presence, or an Essence. We are always struggling to raise ourselves up to that ideal. Every human being, whosoever and wheresoever he may be, has an ideal of infinite power. Every human being has an ideal of infinite pleasure. Most of the works that we find around us, the activities displayed everywhere, are due to the struggle for this infinite power, or this infinite pleasure. But a few quickly discover that although they are struggling for infinite power, it is not through the senses that it can be reached. They find out very soon that that infinite pleasure is not to be got through the senses, or, in other words, the senses are too limited, and the body is too limited, to express the Infinite. To manifest the Infinite through the finite is impossible, and sooner or later, man learns to give up the attempt to express the Infinite through the finite. This giving up, this renunciation of the attempt, is the background of ethics. Renunciation is the very basis upon which ethics stands. There never was an ethical code preached which had not renunciation for its basis.

Ethics always says: 'Not I, but thou.' Its motto is 'Not self, but non-self.' The vain ideas of individualism to which man clings when he is trying to find that Infinite Power or that Infinite Pleasure through the senses, have to be given up—say the laws of ethics. You have to put *yourself* last, and others before you. The senses say, 'Myself first.' Ethics says, 'I must hold myself last.' Thus, all codes of ethics are based upon this renunciation; destruction, not construction, of the individual on the material plane. That Infinite will never find expression upon the material plane, nor is it possible or thinkable.

So man has to give up the plane of matter and rise to other spheres to seek a deeper expression of that Infinite. In this way the various ethical laws are being moulded, but all have that one central idea, eternal self-abnegation. Perfect self-annihilation is the ideal of ethics. People are startled if they are asked not to think of their individualities. They seem so very much afraid of losing what they call their individuality. At the same time, the same men would declare the highest ideals of ethics to be right, never for a moment thinking that the scope, the goal, the idea of all ethics is the destruction, and not the building up, of the individual.

Utilitarian standards cannot explain the ethical relations of men, for, in the first place we cannot derive any ethical laws from considerations of utility. Without the supernatural sanction as it is called, or the perception of the superconscious, as I prefer to term it, there can be no ethics. Without the struggle towards the Infinite, there can be no ideal. Any system that wants to bind men down to the limits of their own societies is not able to find an explanation for the ethical laws of mankind. The Utilitarian wants us to give up the struggle after the Infinite, the reaching-out for the Supersensuous, as impracticable and absurd, and, in the same breath, asks us to take up ethics and do good to society. Why should we do good? Doing good is a secondary consideration. We must have an ideal. Ethics itself is not the end, but the means to the end. If the end is not there, why should we be ethical? Why should I do good to other men, and not injure them? If happiness is the goal of mankind, why should I not make myself happy, and others unhappy? What prevents me? In the second place, the basis of utility is too narrow. All the current social forms and methods are derived from society as it exists, but what right has the Utilitarian to assume that society is eternal? Society did not exist ages ago, possibly will not exist ages hence. Most probably it is one of the passing stages through which we are going towards a higher evolution, and any law that is derived from society alone cannot be eternal, cannot cover the whole ground of man's nature. At best, therefore, Utilitarian theories can only work under present social conditions. Beyond that, they have no value. But a morality, an ethical code, derived from religion and spirituality, has the whole of infinite man for its scope. It takes up the individual, but its relations are to the Infinite, and it takes up society also—because society is nothing but numbers of these individuals grouped together; and as it applies to the individual and *his* eternal relations, it must necessarily apply to the whole of society, in whatever condition it may be at any given time. Thus we see that there is always the necessity of spiritual religion for mankind. Man cannot always think of matter, however pleasurable it may be.

It has been said that too much attention to things spiritual disturbs our practical relations in this world. As far back as in the days of the Chinese sage Confucius, it was said, 'Let us take care of this world: and then, when we have finished with this world, we will take care of other world.' It is all very well that we should *take care* of this world. But if too much attention to the spiritual may affect a little our practical relations, too much attention to the so-called practical hurts us here and hereafter. It makes us materialistic. For man is not to regard *nature* as his goal, but something higher.

Man is man, so long as he is struggling to rise above

nature, and this nature is both internal and external. Not only does it comprise the laws that govern the particles of matter outside us and in our bodies, but also the more subtle nature within, which is, in fact, the motive power governing the external. It is good and very grand to conquer external nature, but grander still to conquer our internal nature. It is grand and good to know the laws that govern the stars and planets; it is infinitely grander and better to know the laws that govern the passions, the feelings, the will, of mankind. This conquering of the inner man, understanding the secrets of the subtle workings that are within the human mind, and knowing its wonderful secrets, belong entirely to religion. Human nature—the ordinary human nature, I mean—wants to see big material facts. The ordinary man cannot understand anything that is subtle. Well has it been said that the masses admire the lion that kills a thousand lambs, never for a moment thinking that it is death to the lambs, although a momentary triumph for the lion; because they find pleasure only in manifestations, of physical strength. Thus it is with the ordinary run of mankind. They understand and find pleasure in everything that is external. But in every society there is a section whose pleasures are not in the senses, but beyond, and who now and then catch glimpses of something higher than matter and struggle to reach it. And if we read the history of nations between the lines, we shall always find that the rise of a nation comes with an increase in the number of such men; and the fall begins when this pursuit after the Infinite, however vain Utilitarians may call it, has ceased. That is to say, the mainspring of the strength of every race lies in its spirituality, and the death of that race begins the day that spirituality wanes and materialism gains ground.

Thus, apart from the solid facts and truths that we may learn from religion, apart from the comforts that we may gain from it, religion, as a science, as a study, is the greatest and healthiest exercise that the human mind can have. This pursuit of the Infinite, this struggle to grasp the Infinite, this effort to get beyond the limitations of the senses—out of matter, as it were—and to evolve the spiritual man—this striving day and night to make the Infinite one with our being—this struggle itself is the grandest and most glorious that man can make. Some persons find the greatest pleasure in eating. We have no right to say that they should not. Others find the greatest pleasure in possessing certain things. We have no right to say they should not. But they also have no right to say 'no' to the man who finds his highest pleasure in spiritual thought. The lower the organisation, the greater the pleasure in the senses. Very few men can eat a meal with the same gusto as a dog or a wolf. But all the pleasures of the dog or the wolf have gone, as it were, into the senses. The lower types of humanity in all nations find pleasure in the senses, while the cultured and the educated find it in thought, in philosophy, in arts and sciences. Spirituality is a still higher plane. The subject being infinite, that plane is the highest, and the pleasure there is the highest for those who can appreciate it. So, even on the utilitarian ground that man is to seek for pleasure, he should cultivate religious thought, for it is the highest pleasure that exists. Thus religion, as a study, seems to me to be absolutely necessary.

We can see it in its effects. It is the greatest motive power that moves the human mind. No other ideal can put into us the same mass of energy as the spiritual. So far as human history goes, it is obvious to all of us that this has been the case and that its powers are not dead. I do not deny that men, on simply utilitarian grounds, can be very good and moral. There have been many great men in this world perfectly sound, moral and good, simply on utilitarian grounds. But the world-movers, men who bring, as it were, a mass of magnetism into the world, whose spirit works in hundreds and in thousands, whose life ignites others with a spiritual fire—such men, we always find, have that spiritual background. Their motive power came from religion. Religion is the greatest motive power for realising that infinite energy which is the birthright and nature of every man. In building up character, in making for everything that is good and great, in bringing peace to others and peace to one's own self, religion is the highest motive power and, therefore, ought to be studied from that standpoint. Religion must be studied on a broader basis than formerly. All narrow, limited, fighting ideas of religion have to go. All sect ideas and tribal or national ideas of religion must be given up. That each tribe or nation should have its own particular God and think that every other is wrong is a superstition that should belong to the

past. All such ideas must be abandoned.

As the human mind broadens, its spiritual steps broaden too. The time has already come when a man cannot record a thought without its reaching to all corners of the earth; by merely physical means, we have come into touch with the whole world; so the future religions of the world have to become as universal, as wide.

The religious ideals of the future must embrace all that exists in the world and is good and great, and, at the same time, have infinite scope for future development. All that was good in the past must be preserved; and the doors must be kept open for future additions to the already existing store. Religions must also be inclusive, and not look down with contempt upon one another, because their particular ideals of God are different. In my life, I have seen a great many spiritual men, a great many sensible persons, who did not believe in God at all, that is to say, not in our sense of the word. Perhaps, they understood God better than we can ever do. The Personal idea of God or the Impersonal, the Infinite, Moral Law, or the Ideal Man—these all have to come under the definition of religion. And when religions have become thus broadened, their power for good will have increased a hundredfold. Religions, having tremendous power in them, have often done more injury to the world than good, simply on account of their narrowness and limitations.

Even at the present time we find many sects and societies, with almost the same ideas, fighting each other, because one does not want to set forth those ideas in precisely the same way as another. Therefore, religions will have to broaden. Religious ideas will have to become universal, vast, and infinite; and then alone we shall have the fullest play of religion, for the power of religion has only just begun to manifest in the world. It is sometimes said that religions are dying out, that spiritual ideas are dying out of the world. To me it seems that they have just begun to grow. The power of religion, broadened and purified, is going to penetrate every part of human life. So long as religion was in the hands of a chosen few or of a body of priests, it was in temples, churches, books, dogmas, ceremonials, forms, and rituals. But when we come to the real, spiritual, universal concept, then, and then alone, religion will become real and living; it will come into our very nature, live in our every movement, penetrate every pore of our society, and be infinitely more a power for good than it has ever been before.

What is needed is a fellow-feeling between the different types of religion, seeing that they all stand or fall together, a fellow-feeling which springs from mutual esteem and mutual respect, and not the condescending, patronising, niggardly expression of goodwill, unfortunately in vogue at the present time with many. And above all, this is needed between types of religious expression coming from the study of mental phenomena—unfortunately, even now laying exclusive claim to the name of religion—and those expressions of religion whose heads, as it were, are penetrating more into the secrets of heaven, though their feet are clinging to earth, I mean, the so-called materialistic sciences.

To bring about this harmony, **both will** have to make concessions, sometimes very large, **nay more**, sometimes painful, but each will find itself the better for the sacrifice and more advanced in truth. And in the end, the knowledge which is confined within the domain of time and space will meet and become one with that which is beyond them both, where the mind and senses cannot reach—the Absolute, the Infinite, the One without a second.

(Complete Works of Swami Vivekananda,
1992, vol. 2, pp. 57–69.)

REASON AND RELIGION

(Evening Class Lecture at 39 Victoria Street, London on November 18, 1896)

A sage called Narada went to another sage named Sanatkumara to learn about truth and Sanatkumara inquired what he had studied already. Narada answered that he had studied the Vedas, Astronomy, and various other things, yet he had got no satisfaction. Then there was a conversation between the two, in the course of which Sanatkumara remarked that all this knowledge of the Vedas, of Astronomy, and of Philosophy, was but secondary; sciences were but secondary. That which made us realise the Brahman was the supreme, the highest knowledge. This idea we find in every religion, and that is why religion always claimed to be supreme knowledge. Knowledge of the sciences covers, as it were, only part of our lives, but the knowledge which religion brings to us is eternal, as infinite as the truth it preaches. Claiming this superiority, religions have many times looked down, unfortunately, on all secular knowledge, and not only so, but many times have refused to be justified by the aid of secular knowledge. In consequence, all the world over there have been fights between secular knowledge and religious knowledge, the one claiming infallible authority as its guide, refusing to listen to anything that secular knowledge has to say on the point, the other, with its shining instrument of reason, wanting to cut to pieces everything religion could bring forward. This fight has been and is still waged in every country. Religions have been again and again defeated, and almost exterminated. The worship of the goddess of Reason during the French Revolution was not the first manifestation of that phenomenon in the history of humanity, it was a re-enactment of what had happened in ancient times, but in modern times it has assumed greater proportions. The physical sciences are better equipped now than formerly, and religions have become less and less equipped. The foundations have been all undermined, and the modern man, whatever he may say in public, knows in the privacy of his heart that he can no more 'believe'. Believing certain things because an organised body of priests tells him to believe, believing because it is written in certain books, believing because his people like him to believe, the modern man knows to be impossible for him. There are, of course, a number of people who seem to acquiesce in the so-called popular faith, but we also know for certain that they do not think. Their idea of belief may be better translated as 'not-thinking-carelessness'. This fight cannot last much longer without breaking to pieces all the buildings of religion.

The question is: Is there a way out? To put it in a more concrete form: Is religion to justify itself by the discoveries of reason, through which every other science justifies itself? Are the same methods of investigation, which we apply to sciences and knowledge outside, to be applied to the science of Religion? In my opinion this must be so, and I am also of opinion that the sooner it is done the better. If a religion is destroyed by such investigations, it was then all the time useless, unworthy superstition; and the sooner it goes the better. I am thoroughly convinced that its destruction would be the best thing that could happen. All that is dross will be taken off, no doubt, but the essential parts of religion will emerge triumphant out of this investigation. Not only will it be made scientific—as scientific, at least, as any of the conclusions of physics or chemistry—but will have greater strength, because physics or chemistry has no internal mandate to vouch for its truth, which religion has.

People who deny the efficacy of any rationalistic investigation into religion seem to me somewhat to be contradicting themselves. For instance, the Christian claims that his religion is the only true one, because it was revealed to so-and-so. The Mohammedan makes the same claim for his religion; his is the only true one, because it was revealed to so-and-so. But the Christian says to the Mohammedan, 'Certain parts of your ethics do not seem to be right. For instance, your books say, my Mohammedan friend, that an infidel may be converted to the religion of Mohammed by force, and if he will not accept the Mohammedan religion he may be killed; and any Mohammedan who kills such an infidel will get a sure entry into heaven, whatever may have been his sins or misdeeds.' The Mohammedan will retort by saying, 'It is right for me to do so, because my book enjoins it. It will be wrong on my part not to do so.' The Christian says, 'But my book does not say so.' The Mohammedan replies, 'I do not know; I am not bound by the authority of your book; my book says, "Kill all the infidels." How do you know which is right and which is wrong? Surely what is written in my book is right and what your book says, "Do not kill," is wrong. You also say the same thing, my Christian friend; you say that what Jehovah declared to the Jews is right to do, and what he forbade them to do is wrong. So say I, Allah declared in my book that certain things should be done, and that certain things should not be done, and that is all the test of right and wrong.' In spite of that the Christian is not satisfied; he insists on a comparison of the morality of the Sermon on the Mount with the morality of the Koran. How is this to be decided? Certainly not by the books, because the books, fighting between themselves, cannot be the judges. Decidedly then we have to admit that there is something more universal than these books, something higher than all the ethical codes that are in the world, something which can judge between the strength of inspirations of different nations. Whether we declare it boldly, clearly, or not—it is evident that here we appeal to reason.

Now, the question arises if this light of reason is able to judge between inspiration and inspiration, and if this light can uphold its standard when the quarrel is between prophet and prophet, if it has the power of understanding anything whatsoever of religion. If it has not, nothing can determine the hopeless fight of books and prophets which has been going on through ages; for it means that all religions are mere lies, hopelessly contradictory, without any constant idea of ethics. The proof of religion depends on the truth of the constitution of man, and not on any books. These books are the outgoings, the effects of man's constitution; man made these books. We are yet to see the books that made man. Reason is equally an effect of that common cause, the constitution of man, where our appeal must be. And yet, as reason alone is directly connected with this constitution, it should be resorted to, as long as it follows faithfully the same. What do I mean by reason? I mean what every educated man or woman is wanting to do at the present time, to apply the discoveries of secular knowledge to religion. The first principle of reasoning is that the particular is explained by the general, the general by the more general, until we come to the universal. For instance, we have the idea of law. If something happens and we believe that it is the effect of such and such a law, we are satisfied; that is an explanation for us. What we mean by that explanation is that it is proved that this one effect, which had dissatisfied us, is only one particular of a general mass of occurrences which we designate by the word 'law'. When one apple fell, Newton was disturbed; but when he found that all apples fell, it was gravitation, and he was satisfied. This is one principle of human knowledge. I see a particular being, a human being, in the street. I refer him to the bigger conception of man, and I am satisfied; I know he is a man by referring him to the more general. So the particulars are to be referred to the general, the general to the more general, and everything at last to the universal, the last concept that we have, the most universal—that of existence. Existence is the most universal concept.

We are all human beings; that is to say, each one of us, as it were, a particular part of the general concept, humanity. A man, and a cat, and a dog, are all animals. These particular examples, as man, or dog, or cat, are parts of a bigger and more general concept, animal. The man, and the cat, and the dog, and the plant, and the tree, all come under the still more general concept, life. Again, all these, all beings, and all materials, come under the one concept of existence, for we all are in it. This explanation merely means referring the particular to a higher concept, finding more of its kind. The mind, as it were, has stored up numerous classes of such generalisations. It is, as it were, full of pigeon-holes where all these ideas are grouped together, and whenever we find a new thing the mind immediately tries to find out its type in one of these pigeon-holes. If we find it, we put the new thing in there and are satisfied, and we are said to have known the thing.

This is what is meant by knowledge, and no more. And if we do not find that there is something like it, we are dissatisfied, and have to wait until we find a further classification for it, already existing in the mind. Therefore, as I have already pointed out, knowledge is more or less classification. There is something more. A second explanation of knowledge is that the explanation of a thing must come from inside and not from outside. There had been the belief that, when a man threw up a stone and it fell, some demon dragged it down. Many occurrences which are really natural phenomena are attributed by people to unnatural beings. That a ghost dragged down the stone was an explanation that was not in the thing itself, it was an explanation from outside; but the second explanation of gravitation is something in the nature of the stone; the explanation is coming from inside. This tendency you will find throughout modern thought; in one word, what is meant by science is that the explanations of things are in their own nature, and that no external beings or existences are required to explain what is going on in the universe. The chemist never requires demons, or ghost, or anything of that sort, to explain his phenomena. The physicist never requires any one of these to explain the things he knows, nor does any other scientist. And this is one of the features of science which I mean to apply to religion. In this religions are found wanting and that is why they are crumbling into pieces. Every science wants its explanations from inside, from the very nature of things; and the religions are not able to supply this. There is an ancient theory of a personal deity entirely separate from the universe, which has been held from the very earliest times. The arguments in favour of this have been repeated again and again, how it is necessary to have a God entirely separate from the universe, an extra-cosmic deity, who has created the universe out of his will, and is conceived by religion to be its ruler. We find, apart from all these arguments, the Almighty God painted as the All-merciful, and the same time, inequalities remain in the world. These things do not concern the philosopher at all, but he says the heart of the thing was wrong; it was an explanation from outside, and not inside. What is the cause of the universe? Something outside of it, some being who is moving this universe! And just as it was found insufficient to explain the phenomenon of the falling stone, so this was found insufficient to explain religion. And religions are falling to pieces, because they cannot give a better explanation than that.

Another idea connected with this, the manifestation of the same principle, that the explanation of everything comes from inside it, is the modern law of evolution. The whole meaning of evolution is simply that the nature of a thing is reproduced, that the effect is nothing but the cause in another form, that all the potentialities of the effect were present in the cause, that the whole of creation is but an evolution and not a creation. That is to say, every effect is a reproduction of a preceding cause, changed only by the circumstances, and thus it is going on throughout the universe, and we need not go outside the universe to seek the causes of these changes; they are within. It is unnecessary to seek for any cause outside. This also is breaking down religion. What I mean by breaking down religion is that religions that have held on to the idea of an extra-cosmic deity, that he is a very big man and nothing else, can no more stand on their feet; they have been pulled down, as it were.

Can there be a religion satisfying these two principles? I think there can be. In the first place we have seen that we have to satisfy the principle of generalisation. The generalisation principle ought to be satisfied along with the principle of evolution. We have to come to an ultimate generalisation, which not only will be the most universal of all generalisations, but out of which everything else must come. It will be of the same nature as the lowest effect; the cause, the highest, the ultimate, the primal cause, must be the same as the lowest and most distant of its effects, a series of evolutions. The Brahman of the Vedanta fulfils that condition, because Brahman is the last generalisation to which we can come. It has no attributes but is Existence, Knowledge and Bliss—Absolute. Existence, we have seen, is the very ultimate generalisation which the human mind can come to. Knowledge does not mean the knowledge we have, but the essence of that, that which is expressing itself in the course of evolution in human beings or in other animals as knowledge. The essence of that knowledge is meant, the ultimate fact beyond, if I may be allowed to say so, even consciousness. That is what is meant by knowledge and what we see in the universe as the essential unity of things. To my mind, if modern science is proving anything again and again, it is this, that we are one—mentally, spiritually, and physically. It is wrong to say we are even physically different. Supposing we are materialists, for argument's sake, we shall have to come to this, that the whole universe is simply an ocean of matter, of which you and I are like little whirlpools. Masses of matter are coming into each whirlpool, taking the whirlpool form, and coming out as matter again. The matter that is in my body may have been in yours a few years ago, or in the sun, or may have been the matter in a plant, and so on, in a continuous state of flux. What is meant by your body and my body? It is the oneness of the body. So with thought. It is an ocean of thought, one infinite mass, in which your mind and my mind are like whirlpools. Are you not seeing the effect now, how my thoughts are entering into yours, and yours into mine? The whole of our lives is one; we are one, even in thought. Coming to a still further generalisation, the essence of matter and thought is their potentiality of spirit; this is the unity from which all have come, and that must essentially be one. We are absolutely one; we are physically one, we are mentally one, and as spirit, it goes without saying, that we are one, if we believe in spirit at all. This oneness is the one fact that is being proved every day by modern science. To proud man it is told; You are the same as that little worm there; think not that you are something enormously different from it; you are the same. You have been that in a previous incarnation, and the worm has crawled up to this man state, of which you are so proud. This grand preaching, the oneness of things, making us one with everything that exists, is the great lesson to learn, for most of us are very glad to be made one with higher beings, but nobody wants to be made one with lower beings. Such is human ignorance, that if anyone's ancestors were men whom society honoured, even if they were brutish, if they were robbers, even robber barons, everyone of us would try to trace our ancestry to them; but if among our ancestors we had poor, honest gentlemen, none of us wants to trace our ancestry to them. But the scales are falling from our eyes, truth is beginning to manifest itself more and more, and that is a great gain to religion. That is exactly the teaching of the Advaita, about which I am lecturing to you. The Self is the essence of this universe, the essence of all souls; He is the essence of your own life, nay, 'Thou art That'. You are one with this universe. He who says he is different from others, even by a hair's breadth, immediately becomes miserable. Happiness belongs to him who knows this oneness, who knows he is one with this universe.

Thus we see that the religion of the Vedanta can satisfy the demands of the scientific world, by referring it to the highest generalisation and to the law of evolution. That the explanation of a thing comes from within itself is still more completely satisfied by Vedanta. The Brahman, the God of the Vedanta, has nothing outside of Himself; nothing at all. All this indeed is He; He is in the universe; He is the universe Himself. 'Thou art the man, Thou art the woman, Thou art the young man walking in the pride of youth, Thou art the old man tottering in his step.' He is here. Him we see and feel; in Him we live, and move, and have our being. You have that conception in the New Testament. It is that idea, God immanent in the universe, the very essence, the heart, the soul of things. He manifests Himself, as it were, in this universe. You and I are little bits, little points, little channels, little expressions, all living inside of that infinite ocean of Existence, Knowledge, and Bliss. The difference between man and man, between angels and man, between man and animals, between animals and plants, between plants and stones is not in kind, because everyone from the highest angel to the lowest particle of matter is but an expression of that one infinite ocean, and the difference is only in degree. I am a low manifestation, you may be a higher, but in both the materials are the same. You and I are both outlets of the same channel, and that is God; as such, your nature is God, and so is mine. You are of the nature of God by your birthright; so am I. You may be an angel of purity, and I may be the blackest of demons. Nevertheless, my birthright is that infinite ocean of Existence, Knowledge, and Bliss. So is yours. You have manifested yourself more today. Wait; I will manifest myself more yet, for I have it all within me. No extraneous explanation is sought; none is asked for. The sum total of this whole universe is God Himself. Is God then matter? No, certainly not, for matter is that God perceived by the five senses; that God as perceived through the intellect is mind; and when the

4

spirit sees, He is seen as spirit. He is not matter, but whatever is real in matter is He. Whatever is real in this chair is He, for the chair requires two things to make it. Something was outside which my senses brought to me, and to which my mind contributed something else, and the combination of these two is the chair. That which existed eternally, independent of the senses and of the intellect, was the Lord Himself. Upon Him the sense are painting chairs, and tables, and rooms, and houses, and worlds, and moons, and suns, and stars, and everything else. How is it, then, that we all see this same chair, that we are all alike painting these various things on the Lord, on this Existence, Knowledge, and Bliss? It need not be that all paint the same way, but those who paint the same way are on the same plane of existence and therefore they see one another's paintings as well as one another. There may be millions of beings between you and me who do not paint the Lord in the same way, and them and their paintings we do not see.

On the other hand, as you all know, the modern physical researches are tending more and more to demonstrate that what is real is but the finer; the gross is simply appearance. However that may be, we have seen that if any theory of religion can stand the test of modern reasoning, it is the Advaita, because it fulfils its two requirements. It is the highest generalisation, beyond even personality, generalisation which is common to every being. A generalisation ending in the Personal God can never be universal, for, first of all, to conceive of a Personal

God we must say, He is all-merciful, all-good. But this world is a mixed thing, some good and some bad. We cut off what we like, and generalise that into a Personal God! Just as you say a Personal God is this and that, so you have also to say that He is not this and not that. And you will always find that the idea of a Personal God has to carry with it a personal devil. That is how we clearly see that the idea of a Personal God is not a true generalisation, we have to go beyond, to the Impersonal. In that the universe exists, with all its joys and miseries, for whatever exists in it has all come from the Impersonal. What sort of a God can He be to whom we attribute evil and other things? The idea is that both good and evil are different aspects, or manifestations of the same thing. The idea that they were two was a very wrong idea from the first, and it has been the cause of a good deal of the misery in this world of ours—the idea that right and wrong are two separate things, cut and dried, independent of each other, that good and evil are two eternally separable and separate things. I should be very glad to see a man who could show me something which is good all the time, and something which is bad all the time. As if one could stand and gravely define some occurrences in this life of ours as good and good alone, and some which are bad and bad alone. That which is good today may be evil tomorrow. That which is bad today may be good tomorrow. What is good for me may be bad for you. The conclusion is, that like every other thing, there is an evolution in good and evil too. There is something which in its evolution, we call, in one degree, good, and in another, evil. The storm that kills my friend I call evil, but that may have saved the lives of hundreds of thousands of people by killing the bacilli in the air. They call it good, but I call it evil. So both good and evil belong to the relative world, to phenomena. The Impersonal God we propose is not a relative God; therefore it cannot be said that It is either good or bad, but that It is something beyond, because It is neither good nor evil. Good, however, is a nearer manifestation of It than evil.

What is the effect of accepting such an Impersonal Being, an Impersonal Deity? What shall we gain? Will religion stand as a factor in human life, our consoler, our helper? What becomes of the desire of the human heart to pray for help to some being? That will all remain. The Personal God will remain, but on a better basis. He has been strengthened by the Impersonal. We have seen that without the Impersonal, the Personal cannot remain. If you mean to say there is a being entirely separate from this universe, who has created this universe just by His will, out of nothing, that cannot be proved. Such a state of things cannot be. But if we understand the idea of the Impersonal, then the idea of the Personal can remain there also. This universe, in its various forms, is but the various readings of the same Impersonal. When we read it with the five senses, we call it the material world. If there be a being with more senses than five, he will read it as something else. If one of us gets the electrical sense, he will see the universe as something else again. There are various forms of that same oneness, of which all these various ideas of worlds are but various readings, and the Personal God is the highest reading that can be attained to, of that Impersonal, by the human intellect. So that the Personal God is true, as much as this chair is true, as much as this world is true, but no more. It is not absolute truth. That is to say, the Personal God is that very Impersonal God and, therefore, it is true, just as I, as a human being, am true and not true at the same time. It is not true that I am what you see I am; you can satisfy yourself on that point. I am not the being that you take me to be. You can satisfy your reason as to that, because light, and various vibrations, or conditions of the atmosphere, and all sorts of motions inside me have contributed to my being looked upon as what I am, by you. If any one of these conditions change, I am different again. You may satisfy yourself by taking a photograph of the same man under different conditions of light. So I am what I appear in relation to your senses, and yet, in spite of all these facts, there is an unchangeable something of which all these are different states of existence, the impersonal me, of which thousands of me's are different persons. I was a child, I was young, I am getting older. Every day of my life, my body and thoughts are changing, but in spite of all these changes, the sum total of them constitutes a mass which is a constant quantity. That is the impersonal me, of which all these manifestations form, as it were, parts.

Similarly, the sum total of this universe is immovable, we know, but everything pertaining to this universe consists of motion, everything is in a constant state of flux, everything changing and moving. At the same time, we see that the universe as a whole is immovable, because motion is a relative term. I move with regard to the chair, which does not move. There must be at least two to make motion. If this whole universe is taken as a unit there is no motion; with regard to what should it move? Thus the Absolute is unchangeable and immovable, and all the movements and changes are only in the phenomenal world, the limited. That whole is Impersonal, and within this Impersonal are all these various persons beginning with the lowest atom, up to God, the Personal God, the Creator, the Ruler of this Universe, to whom we pray, before whom we kneel, and so on. Such a Personal God can be established with a great deal of reason. Such a Personal God is explicable as the highest manifestation of the Impersonal. You and I are very low manifestations, and the Personal God is the highest of which we can conceive. Nor can you or I become that Personal God. When the Vedanta says you and I are God, it does not mean the Personal God. To take an example. Out of a mass of clay a huge elephant of clay is manufactured, and out of the same clay a little clay mouse is made. Would the clay mouse ever be able to become the clay elephant? But put them both in water and they are both clay; as clay they are both one, but as mouse and elephant there will be an eternal difference between them. The Infinite, the Impersonal, is like the clay in the example. We and the Ruler of the Universe are one, but as manifested beings, men, we are His eternal slaves, His worshippers. Thus we see that the Personal God remains. Everything else in this relative world remains, and religion is made to stand on a better foundation. Therefore it is necessary that we first know the Impersonal in order to know the Personal.

As we have seen, the law of reason says, the particular is only known through the general. So all these particulars, from man to God, are only known through the Impersonal, the highest generalisation. Prayers will remain, only they will get a better meaning. All those senseless ideas of prayer, the low stages of prayer, which are simply giving words to all sorts of silly desire in our minds, perhaps, will have to go. In all sensible religions, they never allow prayers to God; they allow prayers to gods. That is quite natural. The Roman Catholics pray to the saints; that is quite good. But to pray to God is senseless. To ask God to give you a breath of air, to send down a shower of rain, to make fruits grow in your garden, and so on, is quite unnatural. The saints, however, who were little beings like ourselves, may help us. But to pray to the Ruler of the Universe, prating every little need of ours, and from our childhood saying, 'Oh Lord, I have a headache; let it go,' is ridiculous. There have been millions of souls that have died in this world, and they are all here; they have become gods and angels; let them come to your help. But God! It cannot be. Unto Him we must go for higher things. A fool indeed is he who, resting on the banks of the Ganga, digs a little well for water; a fool indeed is he who, living near a mine of diamonds, digs for bits of crystal.

And indeed we shall be fools if we go to the Father of

all mercy, Father of all love, for trivial earthly things. Unto Him, therefore, we shall go for light, for strength, for love. But so long as there is weakness and a craving for servile dependence in us, there will be these little prayers and ideas of the worship of the Personal God. But those who are highly advanced do not care for such little helps, they have wellnigh forgotten all about this seeking things for themselves, wanting things for themselves. The predominant idea in them is—not I, but thou, my brother. Those are the fit persons to worship the Impersonal God. And what is the worship of the Impersonal God? No slavery there—'Oh Lord, I am nothing, have mercy on me.' You know the old Persian poem, translated into English: 'I came to see my beloved. The doors were closed. I knocked and a voice came from inside. "Who art thou?" "I am so-and-so." The door was not opened. A second time I came and knocked; I was asked the same question, and gave the same answer. The door opened not. I came a third time, and the same question came. I answered, "I am thee, my love," and the door opened.' Worship of the Impersonal God is through truth. And what is truth? That I am He. When I say that I am not Thou, it is untrue. When I say I am separate from you it is a lie, a terrible lie. I am one with this universe, born one. It is self-evident to my senses that I am one with the universe. I am one with the air that surrounds me, one with heat, one with light, eternally one with the whole Universal Being, who is called this universe, who is mistaken for the universe, for it is He and nothing else, the eternal subject in the heart who says, 'I am,' in every heart—the deathless one, the sleepless one, ever awake, the immortal, whose glory never dies, whose powers never fail. I am one with That.

This is all the worship of the Impersonal, and what is the result? The whole life of man will be changed. Strength, strength it is that we want so much in this life, for what we call sin and sorrow have all one cause, and that is our weakness. With weakness comes ignorance, and with ignorance comes misery. It will make us strong. Then miseries will be laughed at, then the violence of the vile will be smiled at, and the ferocious tiger will reveal, behind its tiger's nature, my own Self. That will be the result. That soul is strong that has become one with the Lord; none else is strong. In your own Bible, what do you think was the cause of that strength of Jesus of Nazareth, that immense, infinite strength which laughed at traitors, and blessed those that were willing to murder him? It was that, 'I and my Father are one'; it was that prayer, 'Father, just as I am one with You, so make them all one with me.' That is the worship of the Impersonal God. Be one with the universe, be one with Him. And this Impersonal God requires no demonstrations, no proofs. He is nearer to us than even our senses, nearer to us than our own thoughts; it is in and through Him that we see and think. To see anything, I must first see Him. To see this wall I first see Him, and then the wall, for He is the eternal subject. Who is seeing whom? He is here in the heart of our hearts. Bodies and minds change; misery, happiness, good and evil come and go; days and years roll on; life comes and goes; but He dies not. The same voice, 'I am, I am,' is eternal, unchangeable. In Him and through Him we know everything. In Him and through Him we see everything. In Him and through Him we sense, we think, we live, and we are. And that 'I,' which we mistake to be a little 'I,' limited, is not only my 'I,' but yours, the 'I' of everyone, of the animals, of the angels, of the lowest of the low. That 'I am' is the same in the murderer as in the saint, the same in the rich as in the poor, the same in man as in woman, the same in man as in animals. From the lowest amoeba to the highest angel, He resides in every soul, and eternally declares, 'I am He, I am He.' When we have understood that voice eternally present there, when we have learnt this lesson, the whole universe will have expressed its secret. Nature will have given up her secret to us. Nothing more remains to be known. Thus we find the truth for which all religions search, that all this knowledge of material sciences is but secondary. That is the only true knowledge which makes us one with this Universal God of the Universe.

(*Complete Works of Swami Vivekananda*
1992, vol. 1, pp. 366–82.)

THE IDEAL OF A UNIVERSAL RELIGION

*How It Must Embrace Different Types of
Minds and Methods*

(Delivered at Hardman Hall, New York on January 12, 1896)

Wheresoever our senses reach, or whatsoever our minds imagine, we find therein the action and reaction of two forces, the one counteracting the other and causing the constant play of the mixed phenomena that we see around us, and of those which we feel in our minds. In the external world, the action of these opposite forces is expressing itself as attraction and repulsion, or as centripetal and centrifugal forces; and in the internal, as love and hatred, good and evil. We repel some things, we attract others. We are attracted by one, we are repelled by another. Many times in our lives we find that without any reason whatsoever we are, as it were, attracted towards certain persons; at other times, similarly, we are repelled by others. This is patent to all, and the higher the field of action, the more potent, the more remarkable, are the influences of these opposite forces. Religion is the highest plane of human thought and life, and herein we find that the workings of these two forces have been most marked. The intensest love that humanity has ever known has come from religion, and the most diabolical hatred that humanity has known has also come from religion. The noblest words of peace that the world has ever heard have come from men on the religious plane, and the bitterest denunciation that the world has ever known has been uttered by religious men. The higher the object of any religion and the finer its organisation, the more remarkable are its activities. No other human motive has deluged the world with blood so much as religion; at the same time, nothing has brought into existence so many hospitals and asylums for the poor; no other human influence has taken such care, not only of humanity, but also of the lowest of animals, as religion has done. Nothing makes us so cruel as religion, and nothing makes us so tender as religion. This has been so in the past, and will also, in all probability, be so in the future. Yet out of the midst of this din and turmoil, this strife and struggle, this hatred and jealousy of religions and sects, there have arisen, from time to time, potent voices, drowning all these noise— making themselves heard from pole to pole, as it were— proclaiming peace and harmony. Will it ever come?

Is it possible that there should ever reign unbroken

harmony in this plane of mighty religious struggle? The world is exercised in the latter part of this century by the question of harmony; in society, various plans are being proposed, and attempts are made to carry them into practice; but we know how difficult it is to do so. People find that it is almost impossible to mitigate the fury of the struggle of life, to tone down the tremendous nervous tension that is in man. Now, if it is so difficult to bring harmony and peace to the physical plane of life—the external, gross, and outward side of it—then a thousand times more difficult is it to bring peace and harmony to rule over the internal nature of man. I would ask you for the time being to come out of the network of words. We have all been hearing from childhood of such things as love, peace, charity, equality, and universal brotherhood; but they have become to us mere words without meaning, words which we repeat like parrots, and it has become quite natural for us to do so. We cannot help it. Great souls, who first felt these great ideas in their hearts, manufactured these words; and at that time many understood their meaning. Later on, ignorant people have taken up those words to play with them and made religion a mere play upon words, and not a thing to be carried into practice. It becomes 'my father's religion,' 'our nation's religion,' 'our country's religion,' and so forth. It becomes only a phase of patriotism to profess any religion, and patriotism is always partial. To bring harmony into religion must always be difficult. Yet we will consider this problem of the harmony of religions.

We see that in every religion there are three parts—I mean in every great and recognised religion. First, there is the philosophy which presents the whole scope of that religion, setting forth its basic principles, the goal and the means of reaching it. The second part is mythology, which is philosophy made concrete. It consists of legends relating to the lives of men, or of supernatural beings, and so forth. It is the abstractions of philosophy concretised in the more or less imaginary lives of men and supernatural beings. The third part is the ritual. This is still more concrete, and is made up of forms and ceremonies, various physical attitudes, flowers and incense, and many other things that appeal to the senses. In these consists the ritual. You will find that all recognised religions have these three elements. Some lay more stress on one, some on another. Let us now take into consideration the first part, philosophy. Is there one universal philosophy? Not yet. Each religion brings out its own doctrines and insists upon them as being the only true ones. And not only does it do that, but it thinks that he who does not believe in them must go to some horrible place. Some will even draw the sword to compel others to believe as they do. This is not through wickedness, but through a particular disease of the human brain called fanaticism. They are very sincere, these fanatics, the most sincere of human beings; but they are quite as irresponsible as other lunatics in the world. This disease of fanaticism is one of the most dangerous of all diseases. All the wickedness of human nature is roused by it.

Anger is stirred up, nerves are strung high, and human beings become like tigers.

Is there any mythological similarity, is there any mythological harmony, any universal mythology accepted by all religions? Certainly not. All religions have their own mythology, only each of them says, 'My stories are not mere myths.' Let us try to understand the question by illustration. I simply mean to illustrate, I do not mean criticism of any religion. The Christian believes that God took the shape of a dove and came down to earth; to him this is history, and not mythology. The Hindu believes that God is manifested in the cow. Christians say that to believe so is mere mythology, and not history, that it is superstition. The Jews think that if an image be made in the form of a box, or a chest, with an angel on either side, then it may be placed in the Holy of Holies; it is sacred to Jehovah; but if the image be made in the form of a beautiful man or woman, they say, 'This is a horrible idol; break it down!' This is our unity in mythology! If a man stands up and says, 'My prophet did such and such a wonderful thing', others will say, 'That is only superstition'; but at the same time they say that their own prophet did still more wonderful things, which they hold to be historical. Nobody in the world, as far as I have seen, is able to make out the fine distinction between history and mythology, as it exists in the brains of the these persons. All such stories, to whatever religion they may belong, are really mythological, mixed up occasionally, it may be, with a little history.

Next come the rituals. One sect has one particular form of ritual and thinks that that is holy, while the rituals of another sect are simply arrant superstition. If one sect worships a peculiar sort of symbol, another sect says, 'Oh, it is horrible!' Take, for instance, a general form of symbol. The phallus symbol is certainly a sexual symbol, but gradually that aspect of it has been forgotten, and it stands now as a symbol of the creator. Those nations which have this as their symbol never think of it as the phallus; it is just a symbol, and there it ends. But a man from another race or creed sees in it nothing but the phallus, and begins to condemn it; yet at the same time he may be doing something which to the so-called phallic worshippers appears most horrible. Let me take two points for illustration, the phallus symbol and the sacrament of the Christians. To the Christians the phallus is horrible, and to the Hindus the Christian sacrament is horrible. They say that the Christian sacrament, the killing of a man and the eating of his flesh and the drinking of his blood to get the good qualities of that man, is cannibalism. This is what some of the savage tribes do; if a man is brave, they kill him and eat his heart, because they think that it will give them the qualities of courage and bravery possessed by that man. Even such a devout Christian as Sir John Lubbock admits this and says that the origin of Christian symbol is in this savage idea. The Christians, of course, do not admit this view of its origin; and what it may imply never comes to their mind. It stands for a holy things, and that is all they want to know. So even in rituals there is no universal symbol, which can command general recognition and acceptance. Where then is any universality? How is it possible then to have a universal form of religion? That, however, already exists. And let us see what it is.

We all hear about universal brotherhood, and how societies stand up especially to preach this. I remember an old story. In India, taking wine is considered very bad. There were two brothers who wished, one night, to drink wine secretly; and their uncle, who was a very orthodox man, was sleeping in a room quite close to theirs. So, before they began to drink, they said to each other, 'We must be very silent, or uncle will wake up.' When they were drinking, they continued repeating to each other, 'Silence! Uncle will wake up', each trying to shout the other down. And, as the shouting increased, the uncle woke up, came into the room, and discovered the whole thing. Now we all shout like these drunken men, 'Universal brotherhood! We are all equal, therefore let us make a sect.' As soon as you make a sect you protest against equality, and equality is no more. Mohammedans talk of universal brotherhood, but what comes out of that in reality? Why, anybody who is not a Mohammedan will not be admitted into the brotherhood; he will more likely have his throat cut. Christians talk of universal brotherhood; but anyone who is not a Christian must go to that place where he will be eternally barbecued.

And so we go on in this world in our search after universal brotherhood and equality. When you hear such talk in the world, I would ask you to be a little reticent, to take care of yourselves, for, behind all this talk is often the intensest selfishness. 'In the winter sometimes a thunder-cloud comes up; it roars and roars, but it does not rain; but in the rainy season the clouds speak not, but deluge the world with water.' So those who are *really* workers, and *really* feel at heart the universal brotherhood of man, do not talk much, do not make little sects for universal brotherhood; but their acts, their movements, their whole life, show out clearly that they in truth possess the feeling of brotherhood for mankind, that they have love and sympathy for all. They do not speak, they *do* and they *live*. This world is too full of blustering talk. We want a little more earnest work, and less talk.

So far we see that it is hard to find any universal features in regard to religion, and yet we know that they exist. We are all human beings, but are we all equal? Certainly not. Who says we are equal? Only the lunatic. Are we all equal in our brains, in our powers, in our bodies? One man is stronger than another, one man has more brain power than another. If we are all equal, why is there this inequality? Who made it? We. Because we have more or less powers, more or less brain, more or less physical strength, it must make a difference between us. Yet, we know that the doctrine of equality appeals to our heart. We are all human beings; but some are men, and some are women. Here is a black man, there is a white man; but all are men, all belong to one humanity. Various are our faces; I see no two alike, yet we are all human beings. Where is this one humanity? I find a man or a woman, either dark or fair; and among all these faces I know that there is an abstract humanity which is common to all. I may not find it when I try to grasp it, to sense it, and actualise it, yet I know for certain that it is there. If I am sure of anything, it is of this humanity which is common to us all. It is through this generalised entity that I see you as a man or a woman. So it is with this universal religion, which runs through all the various religions of the world in the form of God; it must and does exist through eternity. 'I am the thread that runs through all these pearls,' and each pearl is a religion or even a sect thereof. Such are the different pearls, and the Lord is the thread that runs through all of them; only the majority of mankind are entirely unconscious of it.

Unity in variety is the plan of the universe. We are all men, and yet we are all distinct from one another. As a part of humanity I am one with you, and as Mr. so-and-so I am different from you. As a man you are separate from the woman; as a human being you are one with the woman. As a man you are separate from the animal, but as living beings man, woman, animal, and plant are all one; and as existence, you are one with the whole universe. That universal existence is God, the ultimate Unity in the universe. In Him we are all one. At the same time, in manifestation, these differences must always remain. In our work, in our energies, as they are being manifested outside, these differences must always remain. We find then that if by the idea of a universal religion it is meant that one set of doctrines should be believed in by all mankind, it is wholly impossible. It can never be, there can never be a time when all faces will be the same. Again, if we expect that there will be one universal mythology, that is also impossible; it cannot be. Neither can there be one universal ritual. Such a state of things can never come into existence; if it ever did, the world would be destroyed, because variety is the first principle of life. What makes us formed beings? Differentiation. Perfect balance would be our destruction. Suppose the amount of heat in this room, the tendency of which is towards equal and perfect diffusion, gets that kind of diffusion, then for all practical purposes that heat will cease to be. What makes motion possible in this universe? Lost balance. The unity of sameness can come only when this universe is destroyed, otherwise such a thing is impossible. Not only so, it would be dangerous to have it. We must not wish that all of us should think alike. There would then be no thought to think. We should be all alike, as the Egyptian mummies in a museum, looking at each other without a thought to think. It is this difference, this differentiation, this losing of the balance between us, which is the very soul of our progress, the soul of all our thought. This must always be.

What then do I mean by the ideal of universal religion? I do not mean any one universal philosophy, or any one universal mythology, or any one universal ritual held alike by all; for I know that this world must go on working, wheel within wheel, this intricate mass of machinery, most complex, most wonderful. What can *we* do then? We can make it run smoothly, we can lessen the friction, we can grease the wheels, as it were. How? By recognising the natural necessity of variation. Just as we have recognised unity by our very nature, so we must also recognise variation. We must learn that truth may be expressed in a hundred thousand ways, and that each of these ways is true as far as it goes. We must learn that the same thing can be viewed from a hundred different standpoints, and yet be the same thing. Take for instance the sun. Suppose a man standing on the earth looks at the sun when it rises in the morning; he sees a big ball. Suppose he starts on a journey towards the sun and takes a camera with him, taking photographs at every stage of his journey, until he reaches the sun. The photographs of each stage will be seen to be different from those of the other stages; in fact, when he gets back, he brings with him so many photographs of so many different suns, as it would appear; and yet we know that the same sun was photographed by the man at the different stages of his progress. Even so is it with the Lord. Through high philosophy or low, through the most exalted mythology or the grossest, through the most refined ritualism or arrant fetishism, every sect, every soul, every nation, every religion, consciously or unconsciously, is struggling upward, towards God; every vision of truth that man has, is a vision of Him and of none else. Suppose we all go with vessels in our hands to fetch water from a lake. One has a cup, another a jar, another a bucket, and so forth, and we all fill our vessels. The water in each case naturally takes the form of the vessel carried by each of us. He who brought the cup, has the water in the form of a cup; he who brought the jar—his water is in the shape of a jar, and so forth; but, in every case, water, and nothing but water, is in the vessel. So it is in the case of religion; our minds are like these vessels, and each one of us is trying to arrive at the realisation of God. God is like that water filling these different vessels, and in each vessel the vision of God comes in the form of the vessel. Yet He is One. He is God in every case. This is the only recognition of universality that we can get.

So far it is all right theoretically. But is there any way of practically working out this harmony in religions? We find that this recognition that all the various views of religion are true has been very very old. Hundreds of attempts have been made in India, in Alexandria, in Europe, in China, in Japan, in Tibet, and lastly in America, to formulate a harmonious religious creed, to make all religions come together in love. They have all failed, because they did not adopt any practical plan. Many have admitted that all the religions of the world are right, but they show no practical way of bringing them together, so as to enable each of them to maintain its own individuality in the conflux. That plan alone is practical, which does not destroy the individuality of any man in religion and at the same time shows him a point of union with all others. But so far, all the plans of religious harmony that have been tried, while proposing to take in all the various views of religion, have, in practice, tried to bind them all down to a few doctrines, and so have produced more new sects, fighting, struggling, and pushing against each other.

I have also my little plan. I do not know whether it will work or not, and I want to present it to you for discussion. What is my plan? In the first place, I would ask mankind to recognise this maxim, 'Do not destroy.' Iconoclastic reformers do no good to the world. Break not, pull not anything down, but build. Help, if you can; if you cannot, fold your hands and stand by and see things go on. Do not injure, if you cannot render help. Say not a word against any man's convictions so far as they are sincere. Secondly, take man where he stands, and from there give him a lift. If it be true that God is the centre of all religions, and that each of us is moving towards Him along one of these radii, then it is certain that all of us *must* reach that centre. And at the centre, where all the radii meet, all our differences will cease; but until we reach there, differences there must be. All these radii converge to the same centre. One, according to his nature, travels along one of these lines, and another, along another; and if we all push onward along our own lines, we shall surely come to the centre, because 'All roads lead to Rome.' Each of us is naturally growing and developing according to his own nature; each will in time come to know the highest truth, for after all, men must teach themselves. What can you and I do? Do you think you can teach even a child? You cannot. The child teaches himself. Your duty is to afford opportunities and to remove obstacles. A plant grows. Do *you* make the plant grow? Your duty is to put a hedge round it and see that no animal eats up the plant, and there your duty ends. The plant grows of itself. So it is in regard to the spiritual growth of every man. None can teach you; none can make a spiritual man of you. You have to teach yourself; your growth must come from inside.

What can an external teacher do? He can remove the obstructions a little, and there his duty ends. Therefore help, if you can; but do not destroy. Give up all ideas that *you* can make men spiritual. It is impossible. There is no other teacher to you than your own soul. Recognise this. What comes of it? In society we see so many different natures. There are thousands and thousands of varieties of minds and inclinations. A thorough generalisation of them is impossible, but for our practical purpose it is sufficient to have them characterised into four classes. First, there is the active man, the worker; he wants to work, and there is tremendous energy in his muscles and his nerves. His aim is to work—to build hospitals, do charitable deeds, make streets, to plan and to organise. Then there is the emotional man who loves the sublime and the beautiful to an excessive degree. He loves to think of the beautiful, to enjoy the aesthetic side of nature, and adore Love and the God of Love. He loves with his whole heart the great souls of all times, the prophets of religions, and the Incarnations of God on earth; he does not care whether reason can or cannot prove that Christ or Buddha existed; he does not care for the exact date when the Sermon on the Mount was preached, or for the exact moment of Krishna's birth; what he cares for is their personalities, their lovable figures. Such is his ideal. This is the nature of the lover, the emotional man. Then, there is the mystic whose mind wants to analyse its own self, to understand the workings of the human mind, what the forces are that are working inside, and how to know, manipulate, and obtain control over them. This is the mystical mind. Then, there is the philosopher who wants to weigh everything and use his intellect even beyond the possibilities of all human philosophy.

Now a religion, to satisfy the largest proportion of mankind, must be able to supply food for all these various types of minds; and where this capability is wanting, the existing sects all become one-sided. Suppose you go to a sect which preaches love and emotion. They sing and weep, and preach love. But as soon as you say, 'My friend, that is all right, but I want something stronger than this—a little reason and philosophy; I want to understand things step by step and more rationally', they say, 'Get out'; and they not only ask you to get out but would send you to the other place, if they could. The result is that that sect can only help people of an emotional turn of mind. They not only do not help others, but try to destroy them; and the most wicked part of the whole thing is that they will not only *not* help others, but do not believe in their sincerity. Again, there are philosophers who talk of the wisdom of India and the East and use big psychological terms, fifty syllables long, but if an ordinary man like me goes to them and says, 'Can you tell me anything to make me spiritual?', the first thing they would do would be to smile and say, 'Oh, you are too far below us in your reason.

What can you understand about spirituality?' These are high-up philosophers. They simply show you the door. Then there are the mystical sects who speak all sorts of things about different planes of existence, different states of mind, and what the power of the mind can do, and so on; and if you are an ordinary man and say, 'Show me anything good that I can do; I am not much given to speculation; can you give me anything that will suit me?', they will smile and say, 'Listen to that fool; he knows nothing, his existence is for nothing.' And this is going on everywhere in the world. I would like to get extreme exponents of all these different sects, and shut them up in a room, and photograph their beautiful derisive smiles!

This is the existing condition of religion, the existing condition of things. What I want to propagate is a religion that will be equally acceptable to all minds; it must be equally philosophic, equally emotional, equally mystic, and equally conducive to action. If professors from the colleges come, scientific men and physicists, they will court reason. Let them have it as much as they want. There will be a point beyond which they will think they cannot go, without breaking with reason. They will say, 'These ideas of God and salvation are superstitious, give them up!' I say, 'Mr. Philosopher, this body of yours is a bigger superstition. Give *it* up, don't go home to dinner or to your philosophic chair. Give up the body, and if you cannot, cry quarter and sit down.' For religion must be able to show how to realise the philosophy that teaches us that this world is one, that there is but one Existence in the universe. Similarly, if the mystic comes, we must welcome him, be ready to give him the science of mental analysis, and practically demonstrate it before him. And if emotional people come, we must sit, laugh, and weep with them in the name of the Lord; we must 'drink the cup of love and become mad.' If the energetic worker comes, we must work with him, with all the energy that we have. And this combination will be the ideal or the nearest approach to a universal religion. Would to God that all men were so constituted that in their minds *all* these elements of philosophy, mysticism, emotion, and of work were equally present in full! That is the ideal, my ideal of a perfect man. Everyone who has only one or two of these elements of character, I consider 'one-sided'; and this world is almost full of such 'one-sided' men, with knowledge of that one road only in which they move; and anything else is dangerous and horrible to them. To become harmoniously balanced in all these four directions is *my* ideal of religion. And this religion is attained by what we, in India, call Yoga—union. To the worker, it is union between men and the whole of humanity; to the mystic, between his lower and Higher Self; to the lover, union between himself and the God of Love; and to the philosopher, it is the union of *all* existence. This is what is meant by Yoga. This is a Sanskrit term, and these four divisions of Yoga have, in Sanskrit, different names. The man who seeks after this kind of union is called a Yogi. The worker is called the Karma-Yogi. He who seeks the union through love is called the Bhakti-Yogi. He who seeks it through mysticism is called the Raja-Yogi. And he who seeks it through philosophy is called the Jnana-Yogi. So this word Yogi comprises them all.

Now first of all let me take up Raja-Yoga. What is this Raja-Yoga, this controlling of the mind? In this country you are associating all sorts of hobgoblins with the word Yoga, I am afraid. Therefore, I must start by telling you that it has nothing to do with such things. No one of these Yogas gives up reason, no one of them asks you to be hoodwinked, or to deliver your reason into the hands of priests of any type whatsoever. No one of them asks that you should give your allegiance to any superhuman messenger. Each one of them tells you to *cling* to your reason, to hold fast to it. We find in all beings three sorts of instruments of knowledge. The first is instinct, which you find most highly developed in animals; this is the lowest instrument of knowledge. What is the second instrument of knowledge? Reasoning. You find that most highly developed in man. Now in the first place, instinct is an inadequate instrument; to animals, the sphere of action is very limited, and within that limit instinct acts. When you come to man, you see it is largely developed into reason. The sphere of action also has here become enlarged. Yet even reason is still very insufficient. Reason can go only a little way and then it stops, it cannot go any further; and if you try to push it, the result is helpless confusion, reason itself becomes unreasonable. Logic becomes argument in a circle. Take, for instance, the very basis of our perception, matter and force. What is matter? That which is acted upon by force. And force? That which acts upon matter. You see the complication, what the logicians call see-saw, one idea depending on the other, and this again depending on that. You find a mighty barrier before reason, beyond which reasoning cannot go; yet it always feels impatient to get into the region of the Infinite beyond. This world, this universe which our senses feel, or our mind thinks, is but one atom, so to say, of the Infinite, projected on to the plane of consciousness; and within that narrow limit, defined by the network of consciousness, works our reason, and not beyond. Therefore, there must be some other instrument to take us beyond, and that instrument is called inspiration. So instinct, reason, and inspiration are the three instruments of knowledge. Instinct belongs to animals, reason to man, and inspiration to God-men. But in all human beings are to be found, in a more or less developed condition, the germs of all these three instruments of knowledge. To have these mental instruments evolved, the germs must be there. And this must also be remembered that one instrument is a development of the other, and therefore does not contradict it. It is reason that develops into inspiration, and therefore inspiration does not contradict reason, but fulfils it. Things which reason cannot get at are brought to light by inspiration; and they do not contradict reason. The old man does not contradict the child, but fulfils the child. Therefore you must always bear in mind that the great danger lies in mistaking the lower form of instrument to be the higher. Many times instinct is presented before the world as inspiration, and then come all the spurious claims for the gift of prophecy. A fool or a semi-lunatic thinks that the confusion going on in his brain is inspiration, and he wants men to follow him. The most contradictory, irrational nonsense that has been preached in the world, is simply the instinctive jargon of confused lunatic brains trying to pass for the language of inspiration.

The first test of true teaching must be, that the teaching should not contradict reason. And you may see that such is the basis of all these Yogas. We take the Raja-Yoga, the psychological Yoga, the psychological way to union. It is a vast subject, and I can only point out to you now the central idea of this Yoga. We have but one method of acquiring knowledge. From the lowest man to the highest Yogi, all have to use the same method; and that method is what is called concentration. The chemist who works in his laboratory concentrates all the powers of his mind, brings them into one focus, and throws them on the elements; and the elements stand analysed, and thus his knowledge comes. The astronomer has also concentrated the powers of his mind and brought them into one focus; and he throws them on to objects through his telescope; and stars and systems roll forward and give up their secrets to him. So it is in every case—with the professor in his chair, the student with his book—with every man who is working to know. You are hearing me, and if my words interest you, your mind will become concentrated on them; and then suppose a clock strikes, you will not hear it; on account of this concentration; and the more you are able to concentrate your mind, the better you will understand me, and the more I concentrate my love and powers, the better I shall be able to give expression to what I want to convey to you. The more this power of concentration, the more knowledge is acquired, because this is the one and only method of acquiring knowledge. Even the lowest shoeblack, if he gives more concentration, will black shoes better; the cook with concentration will cook a meal all the better. In making money, or in worshipping God, or in doing anything, the stronger the power of concentration, the better will that thing be done. This is the one call, the one knock, which opens the gates of nature, and lets out floods of light. This, the power of concentration, is the only key to the treasure-house of knowledge. The system of Raja-Yoga deals almost exclusively with this. In the present state of our body we are so much distracted, and the mind is frittering away its energies upon a hundred sorts of things. As soon as I try to calm my thoughts, and concentrate my mind upon any one object of knowledge, thousands of undesired impulses rush into the brain, thousands of thoughts rush into the mind and disturb it. How to check it and bring the mind under control is the whole subject of study in Raja-yoga.

Now take Karma-Yoga, the attainment of God through work. It is evident that in society there are many persons who seem to be born for some sort of activity or other, whose minds cannot be concentrated on the plane of thought alone, and who have but one idea, concretised in work, visible and tangible. There must be a science for this kind of life too. Each one of us is engaged in some work, but the majority of us fritter away the greater portion of our energies, because we do not know the secret of work. Karma-Yoga explains this secret and teaches where and how to work, how to employ to the greatest advantage, the largest part of our energies in the work that is before us. But with this secret we must take into consideration the great objection against work, namely, that it causes pain. All misery and pain come from attachment. I want to do work, I want to do good to a human being; and it is ninety to one that that human being whom I have helped will prove ungrateful and go against me; and the result to me is pain. Such things deter mankind from working; and it spoils a good portion of the work and energy of mankind, this fear of pain and misery. Karma-Yoga teaches us how to work for work's sake, unattached, without caring who is helped, and what for. The Karma-Yogi works because it is his nature, because he *feels* that it is good for him to do so, and he has no object beyond that. His position in this world is that of a giver, and he never cares to receive anything. He knows that he is giving, and does not ask for anything in return and, therefore, he eludes the grasp of misery. The grasp of pain, whenever it comes, is the result of the reaction of 'attachment'.

There is then the Bhakti-Yoga for the man of emotional nature, the lover. He wants to love God, he relies upon and uses all sorts of rituals, flowers, incense, beautiful buildings, forms, and all such things. Do you mean to say they are wrong? One fact I must tell you. It is good for you to remember, in this country especially, that the world's great spiritual giants have all been produced only by those religious sects which have been in possession of very rich mythology and ritual. All sects that have attempted to worship God without any form or ceremony have crushed without mercy everything that is beautiful and sublime in religion. Their religion is a fanaticism at best, a dry thing. The history of the world is a standing witness to this fact. Therefore do not decry these rituals and mythologies. Let people have them; let those who so desire have them. Do not exhibit that unworthy derisive smile, and say, 'They are fools; let them have it.' Not so; the greatest men I have seen in my life, the most wonderfully developed in spirituality, have all come through the discipline of these rituals. I do not hold myself worthy to sit at their feet, and for *me* to criticise *them*! How do I know how these ideas act upon the human mind, which of them I am to accept and which to reject? We are apt to criticise everything in the world without sufficient warrant. Let people have all the mythology they want, with its beautiful inspirations; for you must always bear in mind that emotional natures do not care for abstract definitions of the truth. God to them is something tangible, the only thing that is real; they feel, hear, and see Him and love Him. Let them have their God. Your rationalist seems to them to be like the fool, who, when he saw a beautiful statue, wanted to break it to find out of what material it was made. Bhakti-Yoga teaches them how to love, without any ulterior motives, loving God and loving the good

6

because it is good to do so, not for going to heaven, nor to get children, wealth, or anything else. It teaches them that love itself is the highest recompense of love—that God Himself is love. It teaches them to pay all kinds of tribute to God as the Creator, the Omnipresent, Omniscient, Almighty Ruler, the Father and the Mother. The highest phrase that can express Him, the highest idea that the human mind can conceive of Him, is that He is the God of Love. Wherever there is love, it is He. 'Wherever there is any love, it is He, the Lord is present there.' Where the husband kisses the wife, He is there in the kiss; where the mother kisses the child, He is there in the kiss; where friends clasp hands, He, the Lord, is present as the God of Love. When a great man loves and wishes to help mankind, He is there giving freely His bounty out of His love to mankind. Wherever the heart expands, He is there manifested. This is what the Bhakti-Yoga teaches.

We lastly come to the Jnana-Yogi, the philosopher, the thinker, he who wants to go beyond the visible. He is the man who is not satisfied with the little things of this world. His idea is to go beyond the daily routine of eating, drinking, and so on; not even the teaching of thousands of books will satisfy him. Not even all the sciences will satisfy him; at the best, they only bring this little world before him. What else will give him satisfaction? Not even myriads of systems of worlds will satisfy him; they are to him but a drop in the ocean of existence. His soul wants to go beyond all that into the very heart of being, by seeing Reality as It is; by realising It, by being It, by becoming one with that Universal Being. That is the philosopher. To say that God is the Father or the Mother, the Creator of this universe, its Protector and Guide, is to him quite inadequate to express Him. To him, God is the life of his life, the soul of his soul. God is his own Self. Nothing else remains which is other than God. All the mortal parts of him become pounded by the weighty strokes of philosophy and are brushed away. What at last truly remains is God Himself.

Upon the same tree there are two birds, one on the top, the other below. The one on the top is calm, silent, and majestic, immersed in his own glory; the one on the lower branches, eating sweet and bitter fruits by turns, hopping from branch to branch, is becoming happy and miserable by turns. After a time the lower bird eats an exceptionally bitter fruit and gets disgusted and looks up and sees the other bird, that wondrous one of golden plumage, who eats neither sweet nor bitter fruit, who is neither happy nor miserable, but calm, self-centred and sees nothing beyond his Self. The lower bird longs for this condition but soon forgets it, and again begins to eat the fruits. In a little while, he eats another exceptionally bitter fruit, which makes him feel miserable, and he again looks up, and tries to get nearer to the upper bird. Once more he forgets and after a time he looks up, and so on he goes again and again, until he comes very near to the beautiful bird and sees the reflection of light from his plumage playing around his own body, and he feels a change and seems to melt away; still nearer he comes, and everything about him melts away, and at last he understands this wonderful change. The lower bird was, as it were, only the substantial-looking shadow, the reflection of the higher; he himself was in essence the upper bird all the time. This eating of fruits, sweet and bitter, this lower little bird weeping and happy by turns, was vain chimera, a dream: all along, the real bird was there above, calm and silent, glorious and majestic, beyond grief, beyond sorrow. The upper bird is God, the Lord of this universe; and the lower bird is the human soul, eating the sweet and bitter fruits of this world. Now and then comes a heavy blow to the soul. For a time, he stops the eating and goes towards the unknown God, and a flood of light comes. He thinks that this world is a vain show. Yet again the senses drag him down, and he begins as before to eat the sweet and bitter fruits of the world. Again an exceptionally hard blow comes. His heart becomes open again to divine light; thus gradually he approaches God, and as he gets nearer and nearer, he finds his old self melting away. When he has come near enough, he sees that he is no other than God, and he exclaims, 'He whom I have described to you as the Life of this universe, as present in the atom, and in suns and moons—He is the basis of our own life, the Soul of our soul. Nay, thou art That.' This is what this Jnana-Yoga teaches. It tells man that he is essentially divine. It shows to mankind the real unity of being, and that each one of us is the Lord God Himself, manifested on earth. All of us, from the lowest worm that crawls under our feet to the highest beings to whom we look up with wonder and awe—all are manifestations of the same Lord.

Lastly, it is imperative that all these various Yogas should be carried out in practice; mere theories about them will not do any good. First we have to hear about them, then we have to think about them. We have to reason the thoughts out, impress them on our minds, and we have to meditate on them, realise them, until at last they become our whole life. No longer will religion remain a bundle of ideas or theories, nor an intellectual assent; it will enter into our very self. By means of intellectual assent we may today subscribe to many foolish things, and change our minds altogether tomorrow. But true religion never changes. Religion is realisation; not talk, nor doctrine, nor theories, however beautiful they may be. It is being and becoming, not hearing or acknowledging; it is the whole soul becoming changed into what it believes. That is religion.

(*Complete Works of Swami Vivekananda*,
1992, vol. 2, pp. 375–96.)

THE WAY TO THE REALISATION OF A UNIVERSAL RELIGION

(Delivered in the Universalist Church, Pasadena, California, January 28, 1900.)

No search has been dearer to the human heart than that which brings to us light from God. No study has taken so much of human energy, whether in times past or present, as the study of the soul, of God, and of human destiny. However immersed we are in our daily occupations, in our ambitions, in our work, in the midst of the greatest of our struggles, sometimes there will come a pause: the mind stops and wants to know something beyond this world. Sometimes it catches glimpses of a realm beyond the senses, and a struggle to get at it is the result. Thus it has been throughout the ages, in all countries. Man has wanted to look beyond, wanted to expand himself; and all that we call progress, evolution, has been always measured by that one search, the search for human destiny, the search for God.

As our social struggles are represented amongst different nations by different social organisations, so is man's spiritual struggle represented by various religions; and as different social organisations are constantly quarrelling, are constantly at war with one another, so these spiritual organisations have been constantly at war with one another, constantly quarrelling. Men belonging to a particular social organisation claim that the right to live only belongs to them; and so long as they can, they want to exercise that right at the cost of the weak. We know that just now there is a fierce struggle of that sort going on in South Africa. Similarly, each religious sect has claimed the exclusive right to live. And thus we find that though there is nothing that has brought to man more blessings than religion, yet at the same time, there is nothing that has brought more horror than religion. Nothing has made more for peace and love than religion; nothing has engendered fiercer hatred than religion. Nothing has made the brotherhood of man more tangible than religion; nothing has bred more bitter enmity between man and man than religion. Nothing has built more charitable institutions, more hospitals for men, and even for animals, than religion; nothing has deluged the world with more blood than religion. We know, at the same time, that there has always been an undercurrent of thought; there have been always parties of men, philosophers, students of comparative religion who have tried and are still trying to bring about harmony in the midst of all these jarring and discordant sects. As regards certain countries, these attempts have succeeded, but as regards the whole world, they have failed.

There are some religions which have come down to us from the remotest antiquity, which are imbued with the idea that all sects should be allowed to live, that every sect has a meaning, a great idea, embedded within itself, and, therefore it is necessary for the good of the world and ought to be helped. In modern times the same idea is prevailing and attempts are made from time to time to reduce it to practice. These attempts do not always come up to our expectations, up to the required efficiency. Nay, to our great disappointment, we sometimes find that we are quarrelling all the more.

Now, leaving aside dogmatic study, and taking a common-sense view of the thing, we find at the start that there is a tremendous life-power in all the great religions of the world. Some may say that they are ignorant of this, but ignorance is no excuse. If a man says: 'I do not know what is going on in the external world, therefore things that are going on in the external world do not exist', that man is inexcusable. Now, those of you that watch the movement of religious thought all over the world are perfectly aware that not one of the great religions of the world has died; not only so, each one of them is progressive. Christians are multiplying, Mohammedans are multiplying, the Hindus are gaining ground, and the Jews also are increasing, and by their spreading all over the world and increasing rapidly, the fold of Judaism is constantly expanding.

Only one religion of the world—an ancient, great religion—has dwindled away, and that is the religion of Zoroastrianism, the religion of the ancient Persians. Under the Mohammedan conquest of Persia about a hundred thousand of these people came and took shelter in India and some remained in ancient Persia. Those that were in Persia, under the constant persecution of the Mohammedans, dwindled down till there are at most only ten thousand; in India there are about eighty thousand of them, but they do not increase. Of course, there is an initial difficulty; they do not convert others to their religion. And then, this handful of persons living in India, with the pernicious custom of cousin marriage, do not multiply. With this single exception, all the great religions are living, spreading, and increasing. We must remember that all the great religions of the world are very ancient, not one has been formed at the present time, and that every religion of the world owes its origin to the country between the Ganga and the Euphrates; not one great religion has arisen in Europe, not one in America, not one; every religion is of Asiatic origin and belongs to that part of the world. If what the modern scientists say is true, that the survival of the fittest is the test, these religions prove by their still living that they are yet fit for some people. There is a reason why they should live, they bring good to many. Look at the Mohammedans, how they are spreading in some places in Southern Asia, and spreading like fire in Africa. The Buddhists are spreading all over central Asia, all the time. The Hindus, like the Jews, do not convert others; still gradually, other races are coming within Hinduism and adopting the manners and customs of the Hindus and falling into line with them. Christianity, you all know, is spreading—though I am not sure that the results are equal to the energy put forth. The Christians' attempt at propaganda has one tremendous defect—and that is the defect of all Western institutions: the machine consumes ninety per cent of the energy, there is too much machinery. Preaching has always been the business of the Asiatics. The Western people are grand in organisation, social institutions, armies, governments, etc.; but when it comes to preaching religion, they cannot come near the Asiatic, whose business it has been all the time, and he knows it, and he does not use too much machinery.

This then is a fact in the present history of the human race, that all these great religions exist and are spreading and multiplying. Now, there is a meaning, certainly, to this; and had it been the will of an All-wise and All-merciful Creator that one of these religions should exist and the rest should die, it would have become a fact long, long ago. If it were a fact that only one of these religions is true and all the rest are false, by this time it would have covered the whole ground. But this is not so; not one has gained all the ground. All religions sometimes advance— sometimes decline. Now, just think of this: in your own country there are more than sixty millions of people, and only twenty-one millions professing religions of all sorts. So it is not always progress. In every country, probably, if the statistics are taken, you would find that religions are sometimes progressing and sometimes going back. Sects are multiplying all the time. If the claims of a religion that it has all the truth and God has given it all this truth in a certain book were true, why are there so many sects? Fifty years do not pass before there are twenty sects founded upon the same book. If God has put all the truth in certain books, He does not give us those books in order that we may quarrel over texts. That seems to be the fact. Why is it? Even if a book were given by God which contained all the truth about religion, it would not serve the purpose because nobody could understand the book. Take the Bible, for instance, and all the sects that exist amongst Christians; each one puts its own interpretation upon the same text, and each says that it alone understands that text and all the rest are wrong. So with every religion. There are many sects among the Mohammedans and among the Buddhists, and hundreds among the Hindus. Now, I bring these facts before you in order to show you that any attempt to bring all humanity to one method of thinking in spiritual things has been a failure and always will be a failure. Every man that starts a theory, even at the present day, finds that if he goes twenty miles away from his followers, they will make twenty sects. You see that happening all the time. You cannot make all conform to the same ideas; that is a fact, and I thank God that it is so. I am not against any sect. I am glad that sects exist, and I only wish they may go on multiplying more and more. Why? Simply because of this: If you and I and all who are present here were to think exactly the same thoughts, there would be no thoughts for us to think. We know that two or more forces must come into collision in order to produce motion. It is the clash of thought, the differentiation of thought, that awakes thought. Now, if we all thought alike, we would be like Egyptian mummies in a museum looking vacantly at one another's faces—no more than that! Whirls and eddies occur only in a rushing, living stream. There are no whirlpools in stagnant, dead water. When religions are dead, there will be no more sects; it will be the perfect peace and harmony of the grave. But so long as mankind thinks, there will be sects. Variation is the sign of life, and it must be there. I pray that they may multiply so that at last there will be as many sects as human beings, and each one will have his own method, his individual method of thought in religion.

But this thing exists already. Each one of us is thinking in his own way, but his natural course has been obstructed all the time and is still being obstructed. If the sword is not used directly, other means will be used. Just hear what one of the best preachers in New York says: he preaches that the Filipinos should be conquered because that is the only way to teach Christianity to them! They are already Catholics; but he wants to make them Presbyterians, and for this, he is ready to lay all this terrible sin of bloodshed upon this race. How terrible! And this man is one of the greatest preachers of this country, one of the best informed men. Think of the state of the world when a man like that is not ashamed to stand up and utter such arrant nonsense; and think of the state of the world when

an audience cheers him! Is this civilisation? It is the old
blood-thirstiness of the tiger, the cannibal, the savage,
coming out once more under new names, new circumstances. What else can it be? If the state of things is such
now, think of the horrors through which the world passed
in olden times, when every sect was trying by every means
in its power to tear to pieces the other sects. History shows
that. The tiger in us is only asleep; it is not dead. When
opportunities come, it jumps up and, as of old, uses its
claws and fangs. Apart from the sword, apart from
material weapons, there are weapons still more terrible—
contempt, social hatred, and social ostracism. Now, these
are the most terrible of all inflictions that are hurled
against persons who do not think exactly in the same way
as we do. And why should everybody think just as we do?
I do not see any reason. If I am a rational man, I should be
glad they do not think just as I do. I do not want to live in
a grave-like land; I want to be a man in a world of men.
Thinking beings must differ; difference is the first sign of
thought. If I am a thoughtful man, certainly I ought to like
to live amongst thoughtful persons where there are differences of opinion.

Then arises the question: How can all these varieties
be true? If one thing is true, its negation is false. How can
contradictory opinions be true at the same time? This is the
question which I intend to answer. But I will first ask you:
Are all the religions of the world really contradictory? I do
not mean the external forms in which great thoughts are
clad. I do not mean the different buildings, languages,

rituals, books, etc. employed in various religions, but I mean the internal soul of every religion. Every religion has a soul behind it, and that soul may differ from the soul of another religion; but are they contradictory? Do they contradict or supplement each other?—that is the question. I took up the question when I was quite a boy, and have been studying it all my life. Thinking that my conclusion may be of some help to you, I place it before you. I believe that they are not contradictory; they are supplementary. Each religion, as it were, takes up one part of the great universal truth, and spends its whole force in embodying and typifying that part of the great truth. It is, therefore, addition, not exclusion. That is the idea. System after system arises, each one embodying a great idea, and ideals must be added to ideals. And this is the march of humanity. Man never progresses from error to truth, but from truth to truth, from lesser truth to higher truth—but it is never from error to truth. The child may develop more than the father, but was the father inane? The child is the father plus something else. If your present state of knowledge is much greater than it was when you were a child, would you look down upon that stage now? Will you look back and call it inanity? Why, your present stage is the knowledge of the child plus something more.

Then, again, we also know that there may be almost contradictory points of view of the same thing, but they will all indicate the same thing. Suppose a man is journeying towards the sun, and as he advances he takes a photograph of the sun at every stage. When he comes back, he has many photographs of the sun, which he places before us. We see that not two are alike, and yet, who will deny that all these are photographs of the same sun, from different standpoints? Take four photographs of this church from different corners: how different they would look, and yet they would all represent this church. In the same way, we are all looking at truth from different standpoints, which vary according to our birth, education, surroundings, and so on. We are viewing truth, getting as much of it as these circumstances will permit, colouring the truth with our own heart, understanding it with our own intellect, and grasping it with our own mind. We can only know as much of truth as is related to us, as much of it as we are able to receive. This makes the difference between man and man, and occasions sometimes even contradictory ideas; yet we all belong to the same great universal truth.

My idea, therefore, is that all these religions are different forces in the economy of God, working for the good of mankind; and that not one can become dead, not one can be killed. Just as you cannot kill any force in nature, so you cannot kill any one of these spiritual forces. You have seen that each religion is living. From time to time it may retrograde or go forward. At one time, it may be shorn of a good many of its trappings; at another time it may be covered with all sorts of trappings; but all the same, the soul is ever there, it can never be lost. The ideal which every religion represents is never lost, and so every religion is intelligently on the march.

And that universal religion about which philosophers and others have dreamed in every country already exists. It is here. As the universal brotherhood of man is already existing, so also is universal religion. Which of you that have travelled far and wide, have not found brothers and sisters in every nation? I have found them all over the world. Brotherhood already exists; only there are numbers of persons who fail to see this and only upset it by crying for new brotherhoods. Universal religion, too, is already existing. If the priests and other people that have taken upon themselves the task of preaching different religions simply cease preaching for a few moments, we shall see it is there. They are disturbing it all the time, because it is to their interest. You see that priests in every country are very conservative. Why is it so? There are very few priests who lead the people; most of them are led by the people and are their slaves and servants. If you say it is dry, they say it is so; if you say it is black, they say it is black. If the people advance, the priests must advance. They cannot lag behind. So, before blaming the priests—it is the fashion to blame the priest—you ought to blame yourselves. You only get what you deserve. What would be the fate of a priest who wants to give you new and advanced ideas and lead you forward? His children would probably starve, and he would be clad in rags. He is governed by the same worldly laws as you are. 'If you go on,' he says, 'let us march.' Of course, there are exceptional souls, not cowed down by public opinion. They see the truth and truth alone they value. Truth has got hold of them, has got possession of them, as it were, and they cannot but march ahead. They never look backward, and for them there are no people. God alone exists for them, He is the Light before them, and they are following that Light.

I met a Mormon gentleman in this country, who tried to persuade me to his faith. I said, 'I have great respect for your opinions, but in certain points we do not agree—I belong to a monastic order, and you believe in marrying many wives. But why don't you go to India to preach?' Then he was astonished. He said, 'Why, you don't believe in any marriage at all, and we believe in polygamy, and yet you ask me to go to your country!' I said, 'Yes; my countrymen will hear every religious thought wherever it may come from. I wish you would go to India, first, because I am a great believer in sects. Secondly, there are many men in India who are not at all satisfied with any of the existing sects, and on account of this dissatisfaction, they will not have anything to do with religion, and, possibly, you might get some of them.' The greater the number of sects, the more chance of people getting religion. In the hotel, where there are all sorts of food, everyone has a chance to get his appetite satisfied. So I want sects to multiply in every country, that more people may have a chance to be spiritual. Do not think that people do not like religion. I do not believe that. The preachers cannot give them what they need. The same man that may have been branded as an atheist, as a materialist, or what not, may meet a man who gives him the truth needed by him, and he may turn out the most spiritual man in the community. We can eat only in our own way. For instance, we Hindus eat with our fingers. Our fingers are suppler than yours, you cannot use your fingers the same way. Not only the food should be supplied, but it should be taken in your own particular way. Not only must you have the spiritual ideas, but they must come to you according to your own method. They must speak your own language, the language of your soul, and then alone they will satisfy you. When the man comes who speaks my language and gives truth in my language, I at once understand it and receive it for ever. This is a great fact.

Now from this we see that there are various grades and types of human minds and what a task religions take upon them! A man brings forth two or three doctrines and claims that his religion ought to satisfy all humanity. He goes out into the world, God's menagerie, with a little cage in hand, and says, 'God and the elephant and everybody has to go into this. Even if we have to cut the elephant into pieces, he must go in.' Again, there may be a sect with a few good ideas. Its followers say, 'All men must come in!' 'But there is no room for them'. 'Never mind! Cut them to pieces; get them in anyhow; if they don't get in, why, they will be damned.' No preacher, no sect, have I ever met that pauses and asks, 'Why is it that people do not listen to us?' Instead, they curse the people and say, 'The people are wicked.' They never ask: 'How is it that people do not listen to my words? Why cannot I make them see the truth? Why cannot I speak in their language? Why cannot

I open their eyes?' Surely, they ought to know better, and when they find people do not listen to them, if they curse anybody, it should be themselves. But it is always the people's fault! They never try to make their sect large enough to embrace every one.

Therefore we at once see why there has been so much narrow-mindedness, the part always claiming to be the whole; the little, finite unit always laying claim to the infinite. Think of little sects, born within a few hundred years out of fallible human brains, making this arrogant claim of knowing the whole of God's infinite truth! Think of the arrogance of it! If it shows anything, it is this, how vain human beings are. And it is no wonder that such claims have always failed, and, by the mercy of the Lord, are always destined to fail. In this line the Mohammedans were the best off: every step forward was made with the sword—the Koran in the one hand and the sword in the other: 'Take the Koran, or you must die; there is no alternative!' You know from history how phenomenal was their success; for six hundred years nothing could resist them, and then there came a time when they had to cry halt. So will it be with other religions if they follow the same methods. We are such babes! We always forget human nature. When we begin life, we think that our fate will be something extraordinary, and nothing can make us disbelieve that. But when we grow old, we think differently. So with religions. In their early stages, when they spread a little, they get the idea that they can change the minds of the whole human race in a few years, and go on killing and massacring to make converts by force; then they fail, and begin to understand better. We see that these sects did not succeed in what they started out to do, which was a great blessing. Just think if one of those fanatical sects had succeeded all over the world, where would man be today? Now, the Lord be blessed that they did not succeed! Yet, each one represents a great truth; each religion represents a particular excellence—something which is its soul. There is an old story which comes to my mind: There were some ogresses who used to kill people and do all sorts of mischief; but they themselves could not be killed, until someone found out that their souls were in certain birds, and so long as the birds were safe nothing could destroy the ogresses. So, each one of us has, as it were, such a bird, where our soul is; has an ideal, a mission to perform in life. Every human being is an embodiment of such an ideal, such a mission. Whatever else you may lose, so long as that ideal is not lost, and that mission is not hurt, nothing can kill you. Wealth may come and go, misfortunes may pile mountains high, but if you have kept the ideal intact, nothing can kill you. You may have grown old, even a hundred years old, but if that mission is fresh and young in your heart, what can kill you? But when that ideal is lost and that mission is hurt, nothing can save you. All the wealth, all the power of the world will not save you. And what are nations but multiplied individuals? So, each nation has a mission of its own to perform in this harmony of races; and so long as that nation keeps to that ideal, that nation nothing can kill; but if that nation gives up its mission in life and goes after something else, its life becomes short, and it vanishes.

And so with religions. The fact that all these old religions are living today proves that they must have kept that mission intact; in spite of all their mistakes, in spite of all difficulties, in spite of all quarrels, in spite of all the incrustation of forms and figures, the heart of every one of them is sound—it is a throbbing, beating, living heart. They have not lost, any one of them, the great mission they came for. And it is splendid to study that mission. Take Mohammedanism, for instance. Christian people hate no religion in the world so much as Mohammedanism. They think it is the very worst form of religion that ever existed. As soon as a man becomes a Mohammedan, the whole of Islam receives him as a brother with open arms, without making any distinction, which no other religion does. If one of your American Indians becomes a Mohammedan, the Sultan of Turkey would have no objection to dine with him. If he has brains, no position is barred to him. In this country, I have never yet seen a church where the white man and the negro can kneel side by side to pray. Just think of that: Islam makes its followers all equal—so, that, you see, is the peculiar excellence of Mohammedanism. In many places in the Koran you find very sensual ideas of life. Never mind. What Mohammedanism comes to preach to the world is this practical brotherhood of all belonging to their faith. That is the essential part of the Mohammedan religion; and all the other ideas about heaven and of life etc., are not Mohammedanism. They are accretions.

With the Hindus you will find one national idea—spirituality. In no other religion, in no other sacred books of the world, will you find so much energy spent in defining the idea of God. They tried to define the ideal of soul so that no earthly touch might mar it. The spirit must be divine; and spirit understood as spirit must not be made into a man. The same idea of unity, of the realisation of God, the omnipresent, is preached throughout. They think it is all nonsense to say that He lives in heaven, and all that. It is a mere human, anthropomorphic idea. All the heaven that ever existed is now and here. One moment in infinite time is quite as good as any other moment. If you believe in a God, you can see Him even now. We think religion begins when you have realised something. It is not believing in doctrines, nor giving intellectual assent, nor making declarations. If there is a God, have you seen Him? If you say 'no', then what right have you to believe in Him? If you are in doubt whether there is a God, why do you not struggle to see Him? Why do you not renounce the world and spend the whole of your life for this one object? Renunciation and spirituality are the two great ideas of India, and it is because India clings to these ideas that all her mistakes count for so little.

With the Christians, the central idea that has been preached by them is the same: 'Watch and pray, for the Kingdom of Heaven is at hand'—which means, purify your minds and be ready! And that spirit never dies. You recollect that the Christians are, even in the darkest days, even in the most superstitious Christian countries, always trying to prepare themselves for the coming of the Lord, by trying to help others, building hospitals, and so on. So long as the Christians keep to that ideal, their religion lives.

Now, an ideal presents itself to my mind. It may be only a dream. I do not know whether it will ever be realised in this world, but sometimes it is better to dream a dream, than die on hard facts. Great truths, even in a dream are good, better than bad facts. So, let us dream a dream.

You know that there are various grades of mind. You may be a matter-of-fact, common-sense rationalist; you do not care for forms and ceremonies; you want intellectual, hard, ringing facts, and they alone will satisfy you. Then there are the Puritans, the Mohammedans, who will not allow a picture or a statue in their place of worship. Very well! But there is another man who is more artistic. He wants a great deal of art—beauty of lines, and curves, the colours, flowers, forms; he wants candles, lights, and all the insignia and paraphernalia of ritual, that he may see God. His mind takes God in those forms, as yours takes it through the intellect. Then, there is the devotional man, whose soul is crying for God: he has no other idea but to worship God, and to praise Him. Then again, there is the philosopher, standing outside all these, mocking at them. He thinks, 'What nonsense they are! What ideas about God!'

They may laugh at each other, but each one has a

place in this world. All these various minds, all these various types are necessary. If there ever is going to be an ideal religion, it must be broad and large enough to supply food for all these minds. It must supply the strength of philosophy to the philosopher, the devotee's heart to the worshipper; to the ritualist, it will give all that the most marvellous symbolism can convey; to the poet, it will give as much of heart as he can take in, and other things besides. To make such a broad religion, we shall have to go back to the time when religions began and take them all in.

Our watchword, then, will be acceptance, and not exclusion. Not only toleration, for so-called toleration is often blasphemy, and I do not believe in it. I believe in acceptance. Why should I tolerate? Toleration means that I think that you are wrong and I am just allowing you to live. Is it not a blasphemy to think that you and I are allowing others to live? I accept all religions that were in the past, and worship with them all; I worship God with every one of them, in whatever form they worship Him. I shall go to the mosque of the Mohammedan; I shall enter the Christian's church and kneel before the crucifix; I shall enter the Buddhistic temple, where I shall take refuge in Buddha and in his Law. I shall go into the forest and sit down in meditation with the Hindu, who is trying to see the Light which enlightens the heart of everyone.

Not only shall I do all these, but I shall keep my heart open for all that may come in the future. Is God's book finished? Or is it still a continuous revelation going on? It is a marvellous book—these spiritual revelations of the world. The Bible, the Vedas, the Koran, and all other sacred books are but so many pages, and an infinite number of pages remain yet to be unfolded. I would leave it open for all of them. We stand in the present, but open ourselves to the infinite future. We take in all that has been in the past, enjoy the light of the present, and open every window of the heart for all that will come in the future. Salutation to all the prophets of the past, to all the great ones of the present, and to all that are to come in the future!

(*Complete Works of Swami Vivekananda*,
1992, vol. 2, pp. 359–74.)

SOUL, GOD AND RELIGION

*(Delivered at the Unity Hall, Hartford,Connecticut,
New York on March 8, 1895)*

Through the vistas of the past the voice of the
centuries is coming down to us; the voice of the sages of
the Himalayas and the recluses of the forest; the voice that
came to the Semitic races; the voice that spoke through
Buddha and other spiritual giants; the voice that comes
from those who live in the light that accompanied man in
the beginning of the earth—the light that shines wherever
man goes and lives with him for ever—is coming to us
even now. This voice is like the little rivulets that come
from the mountains. Now they disappear, and now they
appear again in stronger flow till finally they unite in one
mighty majestic flood. The messages that are coming
down to us from the prophets and holy men and women
of all sects and nations are joining their forces and
speaking to us with the trumpet voice of the past. And the

first message it brings us is: Peace be unto you and to all religions. It is not a message of antagonism, but of one united religion.

Let us study this message first. At the beginning of this century it was almost feared that religion was at an end. Under the tremendous sledge-hammer blows of scientific research, old superstitions were crumbling away like masses of porcelain. Those to whom religion meant only a bundle of creeds and meaningless ceremonials were in despair; they were at their wit's end. Everything was slipping between their fingers. For a time it seemed inevitable that the surging tide of agnosticism and materialism would sweep all before it. There were those who did not dare utter what they thought. Many thought the case hopeless and the cause of religion lost once and for ever. But the tide has turned and to the rescue has come— what? The study of comparative religions. By the study of different religions we find that in essence they are one. When I was a boy, this scepticism reached me, and it seemed for a time as if I must give up all hope of religion. But fortunately for me I studied the Christian religion, the Mohammedan, the Buddhistic, and others, and what was my surprise to find that the same foundation principles taught by my religion were also taught by all religions. It appealed to me this way. What is the truth? I asked. Is this world true? Yes. Why? Because I see it. Are the beautiful sounds we just heard (the vocal and instrumental music) true? Yes. Because we heard them. We know that man has a body, eyes and ears, and he has a spiritual nature which we cannot see. And with his spiritual faculties he can study these different religions and find that whether a religion is taught in the forests and jungles of India or in a Christian land, in essentials all religions are one. This only shows us that religion is a constitutional necessity of the human mind. The proof of one religion depends on the proof of all the rest. For instance, if I have six fingers, and no one else has, you may well say that is abnormal. The same reasoning may be applied to the argument that only one religion is true and all others false. One religion only, like one set of six fingers in the world, would be unnatural. We see, therefore, that if one religion is true, all others must be true. There are differences in non-essentials, but in essentials they are all one. If my five fingers are true, they prove that your five fingers are true too. Wherever man is, he must develop a belief, he must develop his religious nature.

And another fact I find in the study of the various religions of the world is that there are three different stages of ideas with regard to the soul and God. In the first place, all religions admit that, apart from the body which perishes, there is a certain part or something which does not change like the body, a part that is immutable, eternal, that never dies; but some of the later religions teach that although there is a part of us that never dies, it had a beginning. But anything that has a beginning must necessarily have an end. We—the essential part of us—never had a beginning, and will never have an end. And above us all, above this eternal nature, there is another eternal

Being, without end—God. People talk about the beginning of the world, the beginning of man. The word *beginning* simply means the beginning of the cycle. It nowhere means the beginning of the whole Cosmos. It is impossible that creation could have a beginning. No one of you can imagine a time of beginning. That which has beginning must have an end. 'Never did I not exist, nor you, nor will any of us ever hereafter cease to be,' says the Bhagavad Gita. Wherever the beginning of creation is mentioned, it means the beginning of a cycle. Your body will meet with death, but your soul, never.

Along with this idea of the soul we find another group of ideas in regard to its perfection. The soul in itself is perfect. The Old Testament of the Hebrews admits man perfect at the beginning. Man made himself impure by his own actions. But he is to regain his old nature, his pure nature. Some speak of these things in allegories, fables and symbols. But when we begin to analyse these statements, we find that they all teach that the human soul is in its very nature perfect, and that man is to regain that original purity. How? By knowing God. Just as the Bible says, 'No man can see God but through the Son.' What is meant by it? That seeing God is the aim and goal of all human life. The sonship must come before we become one with the Father. Remember that man lost his purity through his own actions. When we suffer, it is because of our own acts; God is not to be blamed for it.

Closely connected with these ideas is the doctrine— which was universal before the Europeans mutilated it—

the doctrine of reincarnation. Some of you may have heard of and ignored it. This idea of reincarnation runs parallel with the other doctrine of the eternity of the human soul. Nothing which ends at one point can be without a beginning and nothing that begins at one point can be without an end. We cannot believe in such a monstrous impossibility as the beginning of the human soul. The doctrine of reincarnation asserts the freedom of the soul. Suppose there was an absolute beginning. Then the whole burden of this impurity in man falls upon God. The all-merciful Father responsible for the sins of the world! If sin comes in this way, why should one suffer more than another? Why such partiality, if it comes from an all-merciful God? Why are millions trampled underfoot? Why do people starve who never did anything to cause it? Who is responsible? If they had no hand in it, surely, God would be responsible. Therefore the better explanation is that one is responsible for the miseries one suffers. If I set the wheel in motion, I am responsible for the result. And if I can bring misery, I can also stop it. It necessarily follows that we are free. There is no such thing as fate. There is nothing to compel us. What we have done, that we can undo.

To one argument in connection with this doctrine I will ask your patient attention, as it is a little intricate. We gain all our knowledge through experience; that is the only way. What we call experiences are on the plane of consciousness. For illustration: A man plays a tune on a piano, he places each finger on each key consciously. He repeats this process till the movement of the fingers becomes a habit. He then plays a tune without having to pay special attention to each particular key. Similarly, we find in regard to ourselves that our tendencies are the result of past conscious actions. A child is born with certain tendencies. Whence do they come? No child is born with a *tabula rasa*—with a clean, blank page—of a mind. The page has been written on previously. The old Greek and Egyptian philosophers taught that no child came with a vacant mind. Each child comes with a hundred tendencies generated by past conscious actions. It did not acquire these in this life, and we are bound to admit that it must have had them in past lives. The rankest materialist has to admit that these tendencies are the result of past actions, only they add that these tendencies come through heredity. Our parents, grandparents and great-grandparents come down to us through this law of heredity. Now if heredity alone explains this, there is no necessity of believing in the soul at all, because body explains everything. We need not go into the different arguments and discussions of materialism and spiritualism. So far the way is clear for those who believe in an individual soul. We see that to come to a responsible conclusion we must admit that we have had past lives. This is the belief of the great philosophers and sages of the past and of modern times. Such a doctrine was believed in among the Jews. Jesus Christ believed in it. He says in the Bible, 'Before Abraham was, I am.' And in another place it is said: 'This is Elias who is said to have come.'

All the different religions which grew among

different nations under varying circumstances and conditions had their origin in Asia, and the Asiatics understand them well. When they came out from the motherland, they got mixed up with errors. The most profound and noble ideas of Christianity were never understood in Europe, because the ideas and images used by the writers of the Bible were foreign to it. Take for illustration the pictures of the Madonna. Every artist paints his Madonna according to his own pre-conceived ideas. I have been seeing hundreds of pictures of the Last Supper of Jesus Christ, and he is made to sit at a table. Now, Christ never sat at a table; he squatted with others, and they had a bowl in which they dipped bread—not the kind of bread you eat today. It is hard for any nation to understand the unfamiliar customs of other people. How much more difficult was it for Europeans to understand the Jewish customs after centuries of changes and accretions from Greek, Roman, and other sources! Through all the myths and mythologies by which it is surrounded it is no wonder that the people get very little of the beautiful religion of Jesus, and no wonder that they have made of it a modern shop-keeping religion.

To come to our point. We find that all religions teach the eternity of the soul, as well as that its lustre has been dimmed, and that its primitive purity is to be regained by the knowledge of God. What is the idea of God in these different religions? The primary idea of God was very vague. The most ancient nations had different Deities— sun, earth, fire, water. Among the ancient Jews we find numbers of these gods ferociously fighting with each

8

other. Then we find Elohim whom the Jews and the Babylonians worshipped. We next find one God standing supreme. But the idea differed according to different tribes. They each asserted that their God was the greatest. And they tried to prove it by fighting. The one that could do the best fighting proved thereby that its God was the greatest. Those races were more or less savage. But gradually better and better ideas took the place of the old ones. All those old ideas are gone or going into the lumber-room. All those religions were the outgrowth of centuries; not one fell from the skies. Each had to be worked out bit by bit. Next come the monotheistic ideas: belief in one God, who is omnipotent and omniscient, the one God of the universe. This one God is extra-cosmic; he lives in the heavens. He is invested with the gross conceptions of His originators. He has a right side and a left side, and a bird in His hand, and so on and so forth. But one thing we find, that the tribal gods have disappeared for ever, and the one God of the universe has taken their place: the God of gods. Still He is only an extra-cosmic God. He is unapproach-able; nothing can come near Him. But slowly this idea has changed also, and at the next stage we find a God immanent in nature.

In the New Testament it is taught, 'Our Father who art in heaven,'—God living in the heavens separated from men. We are living on earth and He is living in heaven. Further on we find the teaching that He is a God immanent in nature; He is not only God in heaven, but on earth too. He is the God in us. In the Hindu philosophy we find a stage of the same proximity of God to us. But we do not stop there. There is the non-dualistic stage, in which man realises that the God he has been worshipping is not only the Father in heaven, and on earth, but that 'I and my Father are one.' He realizes in his soul that he is God Himself, only a lower expression of Him. All that is real in me is He; all that is real in Him is I. The gulf between God and man is thus bridged. Thus we find how, by knowing God, we find the kingdom of heaven within us.

In the first or dualistic stage, man knows he is a little personal soul, John, James, or Tom; and he says, 'I will be John, James, or Tom to all eternity, and never anything else.' As well might the murderer come along and say, 'I will remain a murderer for ever.' But as time goes on, Tom vanishes and goes back to the original pure Adam.

'Blessed are the pure in heart, for they shall see God.' Can we see God? Of course not. Can we know God? Of course not. If God can be known, He will be God no longer. Knowledge is limitation. But I and my Father are one: I find the reality in my soul. These ideas are expressed in some religions, and in others only hinted. In some they were expatriated. Christ's teachings are now very little understood in this country. If you will excuse me, I will say that they have never been very well understood.

The different stages of growth are absolutely necessary to the attainment of purity and perfection. The varying systems of religion are at bottom founded on the same ideas. Jesus says the kingdom of heaven is within you. Again he says, 'Our Father who art in Heaven.' How do you reconcile the two sayings? In this way: He was talking to the uneducated masses when he said the latter, the masses who were uneducated in religion. It was necessary to speak to them in their own language. The masses want concrete ideas, something the senses can grasp. A man may be the greatest philosopher in the world, but a child in religion. When a man has developed a high state of spirituality he can understand that the kingdom of heaven is within him. That is the real kingdom of the mind. Thus we see that the apparent contradictions and perplexities in every religion mark but different stages of growth. And as such we have no right to blame anyone for his religion. There are stages of growth in which forms and symbols are necessary; they are the language that the souls in that stage can understand.

The next idea that I want to bring to you is that religion does not consist in doctrines or dogmas. It is not what you read, nor what dogmas you believe that is of importance, but what you realise. 'Blessed are the pure in heart, for they shall see God,' yea, in this life. And that is salvation. There are those who teach that this can be gained by the mumbling of words. But no great Master ever taught that external forms were necessary for salvation. The power of attaining it is within ourselves. We live and move in God. Creeds and sects have their parts to play, but they are for children, they last but temporarily. Books never make religions, but religions make books. We must not forget that. No book ever created God, but God inspired all the great books. And no book ever created a soul. We must never forget that. The end of all religions is the realising of God in the soul. That is the one universal religion. If there is one universal truth in all religions, I place it here—in realising God. Ideals and methods may differ, but that is the central point. There may be a thousand different radii, but they all converge to the one centre, and that is the realisation of God: something behind this world of sense, this world of eternal eating and drinking and talking nonsense, this world of false shadows and selfishness. There is that beyond all books, beyond all creeds, beyond the vanities of this world, and it is the realisation of God within yourself. A man may believe in all the churches in the world, he may carry in his head all the sacred books ever written, he may baptise himself in all the rivers of the earth, still, if he has no perception of God, I would class him with the rankest atheist. And a man may have never entered a church or a mosque, nor performed any ceremony, but if he feels God within himself and is thereby lifted above the vanities of the world, that man is a holy man, a saint, call him what you will. As soon as a man stands up and says he is right or his church is right, and all others are wrong, he is himself all wrong. He does not know that upon the proof of all the others depends the proof of his own. Love and charity for the whole human race, that is the test of true religiousness. I do not mean the sentimental statement that all men are brothers, but that one must feel the oneness of human life. So far as they are not exclusive, I see that the sects and creeds are all mine; they are all grand. They are all helping men towards the real religion. I will add, it is good to be born in a church, but it is bad to die there. It is good to be born a child, but bad to remain a child. Churches, ceremonies, and symbols are good for children, but when the child is grown, he must burst the church or himself. We must not remain children for ever. It is like trying to fit one coat to all sizes and growths. I do not deprecate the existence of sects in the world. Would to God there were twenty millions more, for the more there are, there will be a greater field for selection. What I do object to is trying to fit one religion to every case. Though all religions are essentially the same, they must have the varieties of form produced by dissimilar circumstances among different nations. We must each have our own individual religion, individual so far as the externals of it go.

Many years ago, I visited a great sage of our own country, a very holy man. We talked of our revealed book, the Vedas, of your Bible, of the Koran, and of revealed books in general. At the close of our talk, this good man asked me to go to the table and take up a book; it was a book which, among other things, contained a forecast of the rainfall during the year. The sage said, 'Read that.' And I read out the quantity of rain that was to fall. He said, 'Now take the book and squeeze it.' I did so and he said, 'Why, my boy, not a drop of water comes out. Until the water comes out, it is all book, book. So until your religion makes you realise God, it is useless. He who only studies books for religion reminds one of the fable of the ass which carried a heavy load of sugar on its back, but did not know the sweetness of it.'

Shall we advise men to kneel down and cry, 'O miserable sinners that we are!' No, rather let us remind them of their divine nature. I will tell you a story. A lioness in search of prey came upon a flock of sheep, and as she jumped at one of them, she gave birth to a cub and died on the spot. The young lion was brought up in the flock, ate grass and bleated like a sheep, and it never knew that it was a lion. One day a lion came across the flock and was astonished to see in it a huge lion eating grass and bleating like a sheep. At his sight the flock fled and the lion-sheep with them. But the lion watched his opportunity and one day found the lion-sheep asleep. He woke him up and said, 'You are a lion.' The other said, 'No,' and began to bleat like a sheep. But the stranger lion took him to a lake and asked him to look in the water at his own image and see if it did not resemble him, the stranger lion. He looked and acknowledged that it did. Then the stranger lion began to roar and asked him to do the same. The lion-sheep tried his voice and was soon roaring as grandly as the other. And he was a sheep no longer.

My friends, I would like to tell you all that you are mighty as lions.

If the room is dark, do you go about beating your chest and crying, 'It is dark, dark, dark!' No, the only way to get the light is to strike a light, and then the darkness goes. The only way to realise the light above you is to strike the spiritual light within you, and the darkness of sin and impurity will flee away. Think of your higher self, not of your lower.

(*Complete Works of Swami Vivekananda*, 1992, vol. 1, pp. 317–27.)

VEDIC RELIGIOUS IDEALS

(Evening Class Lecture at 39 Victoria Street,
London on October 13, 1896)

What concerns us most is the religious thought—on soul and God and all that appertains to religion. We will take the Samhitas. These are collections of hymns forming, as it were, the oldest Aryan literature, properly speaking, the oldest literature in the world. There may have been some scraps of literature of older date here and there, older than that even, but not books, or literature properly so called. As a collected book, this is the oldest the world has, and herein is portrayed the earliest feeling of the Aryans, their aspirations, the questions that arose about their manners and methods, and so on. At the very outset we find a very curious idea. These hymns are sung in praise of different gods, Devas as they are called, the bright ones. There is quite a number of them. One is called Indra, another Varuna, another Mitra, Parjanya, and so on.

Various mythological and allegorical figures come before us one after the other—for instance, Indra the thunderer, striking the serpent who has withheld the rains from mankind. Then he lets fly his thunderbolt, the serpent is killed, and rain comes down in showers. The people are pleased, and they worship Indra with oblations. They make a sacrificial pyre, kill some animals, roast their flesh upon spits, and offer that meat to Indra. And they had a popular plant called Soma. What plant it was nobody knows now; it has entirely disappeared, but from the books we gather that, when crushed, it produced a sort of milky juice, and that was fermented; and it can also be gathered that this fermented Soma juice was intoxicating. This also they offered to Indra and the other gods, and they also drank it themselves. Sometimes they drank a little too much, and so did the gods. Indra on occasions got drunk. There are passages to show that Indra at one time drank so much of this Soma juice that he talked irrelevant words. So with Varuna. He is another god, very powerful, and is in the same way protecting his votaries, and they are praising him with their libations of Soma. So is the god of war, and so on. But the popular idea that strikes one as making the mythologies of the Samhitas entirely different from the other mythologies is, that along with every one of these gods is the idea of infinity. This infinite is abstracted, and sometimes described as Āditya. At other times it is affixed, as it were, to all the other gods. Take, for example, Indra. In some of the books you will find that Indra has a body, is very strong, sometimes is wearing golden armour, and comes down, lives and eats with his votaries, fights the demons, fights the snakes, and so on. Again, in one hymn we find that Indra has been given a very high position; he is omnipresent and omnipotent, and Indra sees the heart of every being. So with Varuna. This Varuna is god of the air, and in charge of the water, just as Indra was previously; and then, all of a sudden, we find him raised up and said to be omnipresent, omnipotent, and so on. I will read one passage about Varuna in his highest form, and you will understand what I mean. It has been translated into English poetry, so it is better that I read it in that form.

The mighty Lord on high our deeds, as if at hand,
    espies;
The gods know all men do, though men would fain
    their acts disguise;
Whoever stands, whoever moves, or steals from place
    to place,
Or hides him in his secret cell—the gods his
    movements trace.
Wherever two together plot, and deem they are alone,
King Varuna is there, a third, and all their schemes
    are known.
This earth is his, to him belong those vast and
    boundless skies;
Both seas within him rest, and yet in that small pool
    he lies,
Whoever far beyond the sky should think his way to
    wing.

He could not there elude the grasp of Varuna the
       King.
His spies, descending from the skies, glide all this
       world around;
Their thousand eyes all-scanning sweep to earth's
       remotest bound.

So we can multiply examples about the other gods;
they all come, one after the other, to share the same fate—
they first begin as gods, and then they are raised to this
conception as the Being in whom the whole universe
exists, who sees every heart, who is the ruler of the
universe. And in the case of Varuna, there is another idea,
just the germ of one idea which came, but was immediately suppressed by the Aryan mind, and that was the idea
of fear. In another place we read they are afraid they have
sinned and asked Varuna for pardon. These ideas were
never allowed, for reasons you will come to understand
later on, to grow on Indian soil, but the germs were there
sprouting, the idea of fear, and the idea of sin. This is the
idea, as you all know, of what is called monotheism. This
monotheism, we see, came to India at a very early period.
Throughout the Samhitas, in the first and oldest part, this
monotheistic idea prevails, but we shall find that it did not
prove sufficient for the Aryans; they threw it aside, as it
were, as a very primitive sort of idea and went further on,
as we Hindus think. Of course in reading books and
criticisms on the Vedas written by Europeans, the Hindu
cannot help smiling when he reads, that the writings of

our authors are saturated with this previous education alone. Persons who have sucked in as their mother's milk the idea that the highest ideal of God is the idea of a Personal God, naturally dare not think on the lines of these ancient thinkers of India, when they find that just after the Samhitas, the monotheistic idea with which the Samhita portion is replete was thought by the Aryans to be useless and not worthy of philosophers and thinkers, and that they struggled hard for a more philosophical and transcendental idea. The monotheistic idea was much too human for them, although they gave it such descriptions as 'The whole universe rests in Him,' and 'Thou art the keeper of all hearts.' The Hindus were bold, to their great credit be it said, bold thinkers in all their ideas, so bold that one spark of their thought frightens the so-called bold thinkers of the West. Well has it been said by Prof. Max Müller about these thinkers that they climbed up to heights where their lungs only could breathe, and where those of other beings would have burst. These brave people followed reason wherever it led them, no matter at what cost, never caring if all their best superstitions were smashed to pieces, never caring what society would think about them, or talk about them; but what they thought was right and true, they preached and they talked.

Before going into all these speculations of the ancient Vedic sages, we will first refer to one or two very curious instances in the Vedas. The peculiar fact—that these gods are taken up, as it were, one after the other, raised and sublimated, till each has assumed the proportions of the infinite Personal God of the Universe—calls for an explanation. Prof. Max Müller creates for it a new name, as he thinks it peculiar to the Hindus; he calls it 'Henotheism.' We need not go far for the explanation. It is within the book. A few steps from the very place where we find those gods being raised and sublimated, we find the explanation also. The question arises how the Hindu mythologies should be so unique, so different from all others. In Babylonian or Greek mythologies we find one god struggling upwards, and he assumes a position and remains there, while the other gods die out. Of all the Molochs, Jehovah becomes supreme, and the other Molochs are forgotten, lost for ever; he is the God of gods. So, too, of all the Greeks gods, Zeus comes to the front and assumes big proportions, becomes the God of the Universe, and all the other gods become degraded into minor angels. This fact was repeated in later times. The Buddhists and the Jains raised one of their prophets to the Godhead, and all the other gods they made subservient to Buddha, or to Jina. This is the world-wide process, but there we find an exception, as it were. One god is praised, and for the time being it is said that all the other gods obey his commands, and the very one who is said to be raised up by Varuna, is himself raised up, in the next book, to the highest position. They occupy the position of the Personal God in turns. But the explanation is there in the book, and it is a grand explanation, one that has given the theme to all subsequent thought in India, and one that will be the theme of the whole world of religions: 'Ekam Sat Vipra Bahudha

Vadanti—That which exists is One; sages call It by various names.' In all these cases where hymns were written about all these gods, the Being perceived was one and the same; it was the perceiver who made the difference. It was the hymnist, the sage, the poet, who sang in different languages and different words, the praise of one and the same Being. 'That which exists is One; sages call It by various names.' Tremendous results have followed from that one verse. Some of you, perhaps, are surprised to think that India is the only country where there never has been a religious persecution, where never was any man disturbed for his religious faith. Theists or atheists, monists, dualists, monotheists are there and always live unmolested. Materialists were allowed to preach from the steps of Brahminical temples, against the gods, and against God Himself; they went preaching all over the land that the idea of God was a mere superstition, and that gods, and Vedas, and religion were simply superstitions invented by the priests for their own benefit, and they were allowed to do this unmolested. And so, wherever he went, Buddha tried to pull down every old thing sacred to the Hindus to the dust, and Buddha died of ripe old age. So did the Jains, who laughed at the idea of God. 'How can it be that there is a God?' they asked; 'it must be a mere superstition.' So on, endless examples there are. Before the Mohammedan wave came into India, it was never known what religious persecution was; the Hindus had only experienced it as made by foreigners on themselves. And even now it is a patent fact how much Hindus have helped to build Christian churches, and how much readiness there is to help them. There never has been bloodshed. Even heterodox religions that have come out of India have been likewise affected; for instance, Buddhism. Buddhism is a great religion in some respects, but to confuse Buddhism with Vedanta is without meaning; anyone may mark just the difference that exists between Christianity and the Salvation Army. There are great and good points in Buddhism, but these great points fell into hands which were not able to keep them safe. The jewels which came from philosophers fell into the hands of mobs, and the mobs took up their ideas. They had a great deal of enthusiasm, some marvellous ideas, great and humanitarian ideas, but, after all, there is something else that is necessary—thought and intellect—to keep everything safe. Wherever you see the most humanitarian ideas fall into the hands of the multitude, the first result, you may notice, is degradation. It is learning and intellect that keep things sure. Now this Buddhism went as the first missionary religion to the world, penetrated the whole of the civilised world as it existed at that time, and never was a drop of blood shed for that religion. We read how in China the Buddhist missionaries were persecuted, and thousands were massacred by two or three successive emperors, but after that, fortune favoured the Buddhists, and one of the emperors offered to take vengeance on the persecutors, but the missionaries refused. All that we owe to this one verse. That is why I want you to remember it. 'Whom they call Indra, Mitra, Varuna—That which exists is One; sages call It by various names.'

It was written, nobody knows at what date, it may be 8,000 years ago, in spite of all modern scholars may say, it may be 9,000 years ago. Not one of these religious speculations is of modern date, but they are as fresh today as they were when they were written, or rather, fresher, for at that distant date man was not so civilised as we know him now. He had not learnt to cut his brother's throat because he differed a little in thought from himself; he had not deluged the world in blood, he did not become demon to his own brother. In the name of humanity he did not massacre whole lots of mankind then. Therefore these words come to us today very fresh, as great stimulating, life-giving words, much fresher than they were when they were written: 'That which exists is One; sages call It by various names.' We have to learn yet that all religions, under whatever name they may be called, either Hindu, Buddhist, Mohammedan, or Christian, have the same God, and he who derides any one of these derides his own God.

That was the solution they arrived at. But, as I have said, this ancient monotheistic idea did not satisfy the Hindu mind. It did not go far enough, it did not explain the visible world: a ruler of the world does not explain the world—certainly not. A ruler of the universe does not explain the universe, and much less an external ruler, one outside of it. He may be a moral guide, the greatest power in the universe, but that is no explanation of the universe; and the first question that we find now arising, assuming proportions, is the question about the universe: 'Whence it come?' 'How did it come?' 'How does it exist?' Various hymns are to be found on this question struggling forward to assume form, and nowhere do we find it so poetically, so wonderfully expressed as in the following hymn:

'Then there was neither aught nor naught, nor air, nor sky, nor anything. What covered all? Where rested all? Then death was not, nor deathlessness, nor change to night and day.' The translation loses a good deal of the poetical beauty. 'Then death was not, nor deathlessness, nor change to night and day;' the very sound of the Sanskrit is musical. '*That* existed, that breath, covering as it were, that God's existence; but it did not begin to move.' It is good to remember this one idea, that it existed, motionless, because we shall find how this idea sprouts up afterwards in the cosmology, how according to the Hindu metaphysics and philosophy, this whole universe is a mass of vibrations, as it were, motions; and there are periods when this whole mass of motions subsides and becomes finer and finer, remaining in that state for some time. That is the state described in this hymn. It existed unmoved, without vibration, and when this creation began, this began to vibrate and all this creation came out of it, that one breath, calm, self-sustained, naught else beyond it.

'Gloom existed first.' Those of you who have ever been in India or any tropical country, and have seen the bursting of the monsoon, will understand the majesty of these words. I remember three poets' attempts to picture this. Milton says, 'No light, but rather darkness visible.' Kalidasa says, 'Darkness which can be penetrated with a needle,' but none comes near this Vedic description, 'Gloom hidden in gloom.' Everything is parching and sizzling, the whole creation seems to be burning away, and for days it has been so, when one afternoon there is in one corner of the horizon a speck of cloud, and in less than half an hour it has extended unto the whole earth, until, as it were, it is covered with cloud, cloud over cloud, and then it bursts into a tremendous deluge of rain. The cause of creation was described as will. That which existed at first became changed into will, and this will began to manifest itself as desire. This also we ought to remember, because we find that this idea of desire is said to be the cause of all we have. This idea of will has been the corner-stone of both the Buddhist and the Vedantic system, and later on, has penetrated into German philosophy and forms the basis of Schopenhauer's system of philosophy. It is here we first hear of it.

'Now first arose desire, the primal seed of mind.
Sages, searching in their hearts by wisdom, found the bond,
Between existence and non-existence.'

It is a very peculiar expression; the poet ends by saying that 'perhaps He even does not know.' We find in this hymn, apart from its poetical merits, that this questioning about the universe has assumed quite definite proportions, and that the minds of these sages must have advanced to such a state, when all sorts of common answers would not satisfy them. We find that they were not even satisfied with this Governor above. There are various other hymns where the same idea comes in, about how this all came, and just as we have seen, when they were trying to find a Governor of the universe, a Personal God, they were taking up one Deva after another, raising him up to that position, so now we shall find that in various hymns one or other idea is taken up, and expanded infinitely and made responsible for everything in the universe. One particular idea is taken as the support, in which everything rests and exists, and that support has become all this. So on with various ideas. They tried this method with Prana, the life principle. They expanded the idea of the life principle until it became universal and infinite. It is the life principle that is supporting everything; not only the human body, but it is the light of the sun and the moon, it is the power moving everything, the universal motive energy. Some of these attempts are very beautiful, very poetical. Some of them as, 'He ushers the beautiful morning,' are marvellously lyrical in the way they picture things. Then this very desire, which, as we have just read, arose as the first primal germ of creation, began to be stretched out, until it became the universal God. But none of these ideas satisfied.

Here the idea is sublimated and finally abstracted into a personality. 'He alone existed in the beginning; He is the one Lord of all that exists; He supports this universe; He who is the author of souls, He who is the author of strength, whom all the gods worship, whose shadow is life, whose shadow is death; whom else shall we worship?

Whose glory the snow-tops of the Himalayas declare, whose glory the oceans with all their waters proclaim.' So on it goes, but, as I told you just now, this idea did not satisfy them.

At last we find a very peculiar position. The Aryan mind had so long been seeking an answer to the question from outside. They questioned everything they could find, the sun, the moon, and stars, and they found all they could in this way. The whole of nature at best could teach them only of a personal Being who is the Ruler of the universe; it could teach nothing further. In short, out of the external world we can only get the idea of an architect, that which is called the Design Theory. It is not a very logical argument, as we all know; there is something childish about it, yet it is the only little bit of anything we can know about God from the external world, that this world required a builder. But this is no explanation of the universe. The materials of this world were before Him, and this God wanted all these materials, and the worst objection is that He must be limited by the materials. The builder could not have made a house without the materials of which it is composed. Therefore he was limited by the materials; he could only do what the materials enabled him to. Therefore the God that the Design Theory gives is at best only an architect, and a limited architect of the universe; He is bound and restricted by the materials; He is not independent at all. That much they had found out already, and many other minds would have rested at that. In other countries the same thing happened; the human mind could not rest there; the thinking, grasping minds wanted to go further, but those that were backward got hold of them and did not allow them to grow. But fortunately these Hindu sages were not the people to be knocked on the head; they wanted to get a solution, and now we find that they were leaving the external for the internal. The first thing that struck them was, that it is not with the eyes and the senses that we perceive that external world, and know anything about religion; the first idea, therefore, was to find the deficiency, and that deficiency was both physical and moral, as we shall see. You do not know, says one of these sages, the cause of this universe; there has arisen a tremendous difference between you and me—why? Because you have been talking sense things and are satisfied with sense-objects and with the mere ceremonials of religion, while I have known the Purusha beyond.

Along with this progress of spiritual ideas that I am trying to trace for you, I can only hint to you a little about the other factor in the growth, for that has nothing to do with our subject, therefore I need not enlarge upon it—the growth of rituals. As those spiritual ideas progressed in arithmetical progression, so the ritualistic ideas progressed in geometrical progression. The old superstitions had by this time developed into a tremendous mass of rituals, which grew and grew till it almost killed the Hindu life. And it is still there, it has got hold of and permeated every portion of our life and made us born slaves. Yet, as the same time, we find a fight against this advance of ritual from the very earliest days. The one objection raised there is this, that love for ceremonials, dressing at certain times, eating in a certain way, and shows and mummeries of religion like these are only external religion, because you are satisfied with the senses and do not want to go beyond them. This is a tremendous difficulty with us, with every human being. At best when we want to hear of spiritual things our standard is the senses; or a man hears things about philosophy, and God, and transcendental things, and after hearing about them for days, he asks: After all, how much money will they bring, how much sense-enjoyment will they bring? For his enjoyment is only in the senses, quite naturally. But that satisfaction in the senses, says our sage, is one of the causes which have spread the veil between truth and ourselves. Devotion to ceremonials, satisfaction in the senses, and forming various theories, have drawn a veil between ourselves and truth. This is another great landmark, and we shall have to trace this ideal to the end, and see how it developed later on into that wonderful theory of Maya of the Vedanta, how this veil will be the real explanation of the Vedanta, how the truth was there all the time, it was only this veil that had covered it.

Thus we find that the minds of these ancient Aryan thinkers had begun a new theme. They found out that in the external world no search would give an answer to their question. They might seek in the external world for ages, but there would be no answer to their questions. So they fell back upon this other method; and according to this, they were taught that these desires of the senses, desires for ceremonials and externalities have caused a veil to come between themselves and the truth, and that this cannot be removed by any ceremonial. They had to fall back on their own minds, and analyse the mind to find the truth in themselves. The outside world failed and they turned back upon the inside world, and then it became the real philosophy of the Vedanta; from here the Vedanta philosophy begins. It is the foundation-stone of the Vedanta philosophy. As we go on, we find that all its inquiries are inside. From the very outset they seemed to declare— look not for the truth in any religion; it is here in the human soul, the miracle of all miracles—in the human soul, the emporium of all knowledge, the mine of all existence—seek here. What is not here cannot be there. And they found out step by step that that which is external is but a dull reflection at best of that which is inside. We shall see how they took, as it were, this old idea of God, the Governor of the universe, who is external to the universe, and first put Him inside the universe. He is not a God outside, but He is inside; and they took Him from there into their own hearts. Here He is in the heart of man, the Soul of our souls, the Reality in us..

Several great ideas have to be understood, in order to grasp properly the workings of the Vedanta philosophy. In the first place it is not philosophy in the sense we speak of the philosophy of Kant and Hegel. It is not one book, or the work of one man. Vedanta is the name of a series of books written at different times. Sometimes in one of these productions there will be fifty different things. Neither are they properly arranged; the thoughts, as it were, have been jotted down. Sometimes in the midst of other extraneous things, we find some wonderful idea. But one fact is remarkable, that these ideas in the Upanishads would be always progressing. In that crude old language, the working of the mind of every one of the sages has been, as it were, painted just as it went; how the ideas are at first very crude, and they become finer and finer till they reach the goal of the Vedanta, and this goal assumes a philosophical name. Just at first it was a search after the Devas, the bright ones, and then it was the origin of the universe, and the very same search is getting another name, more philosophical, clearer—the unity of all things —'Knowing which everything else becomes known.'

(*Complete Works of Swami Vivekananda,*
1992, vol. 1, pp. 344–56.)

THE HINDU RELIGION

My religion is to learn. I read my Bible better in the light of your Bible and the dark prophecies of my religion become brighter when compared with those of your prophets. Truth has always been universal. If I alone were to have six fingers on my hand while all of you had only five, you would not think that my hand was the true intent of Nature, but rather that it was abnormal and diseased. Just so with religion. If one creed alone were to be true and all the others untrue, you would have a right to say that that religion was diseased; if one religion is true, all the others must be true. Thus the Hindu religion is your property as well as mine. Of the two hundred and ninety millions of people inhabiting India, only two millions are Christians, sixty millions Mohammedans and all the rest are Hindus.

The Hindus found their creed upon the ancient Vedas, a word derived from Vid, 'to know.' These are a series of books, which, to our minds, contain the essence of all religion; but we do not think they alone contain the truths. They teach us the immortality of the soul. In every country and in every human breast there is a natural desire to find a stable equilibrium—something that does not change. We cannot find it in Nature, for all the universe is nothing but an infinite mass of changes. But to infer from that that nothing unchanging exists is to fall into the error of the Southern school of Buddhists and the Charvakas, which latter believe that all is matter and nothing mind, that all religion is a cheat, and morality and goodness, useless superstitions. The Vedanta philosophy teaches that man is not bound by his five senses. They only know the present, and neither the future nor the past; but as the present signifies both past and future, and all three are only demarcations of time, the present also would be unknown if it were not for something above the senses, something independent of time, which unifies the past and the future in the present.

But what is independent? Not our body, for it depends upon outward conditions; nor our mind, because the thoughts of which it is composed are caused. It is our soul. The Vedas say the whole world is a mixture of independence and dependence, of freedom and slavery, but through it all shines the soul independent, immortal, pure, perfect, holy. For if it is independent, it cannot perish, as death is but a change, and depends upon conditions; if independent, it must be perfect, for imperfection is again but a condition, and therefore dependent. And this immortal and perfect soul must be the same in the highest God as well as in the humblest man, the difference between them being only in the degree in which this soul manifests itself.

But why should the soul take to itself a body? For the same reason that I take a looking-glass—to see myself. Thus, in the body, the soul is reflected. The soul is God, and every human being has a perfect divinity within him-self, and each one must show his divinity sooner or later. If I am in a dark room, no amount of protestation will make it any brighter—I must light a match. Just so, no amount of grumbling and wailing make our imperfect body more perfect. But the Vedanta teaches—call forth your soul, show your divinity. Teach your children that they are divine, that religion is a positive something and not a negative nonsense; that it is not subjection to groans when under oppression, but expansion and manifestation.

Every religion has it that man's present and future are modified by the past, and that the present is but the effect of the past. How is it, then, that every child is born with an experience that cannot be accounted for by hereditary transmission? How is it that one is born of good parents, receives a good education and becomes a good man, while another comes from besotted parents and ends on the gallows? How do you explain this inequality without implicating God? Why should a merciful Father set His child in such conditions which must bring forth misery? It is no explanation to say God will make amends later on—God has no blood-money. Then, too, what becomes of my liberty, if this be my first birth? Coming into this world without the experience of a former life, my independence would be gone, for my path would be marked out by the experience of others. If I cannot be the maker of my own fortune, then I am not free. I take upon myself the blame for the misery of this existence, and say I will unmake the evil I have done in another existence. This, then, is our philosophy of the migration of the soul. We come into this life with the experience of another, and the fortune or misfortune of this existence is the result of our acts in a former existence, always becoming better, till at last perfection is reached.

We believe in a God, the Father of the universe, infinite and omnipotent. But if our soul at last becomes perfect, it also must become infinite. But there is no room for two infinite unconditional beings, and hence we believe in a Personal God, and we ourselves are He. These are the three stages which every religion has taken. First we see God in the far beyond, then we come nearer to Him and give Him omnipresence so that we live in Him; and at last we recognise that we are He. The idea of an objective God is not untrue—in fact, every idea of God, and hence every religion, is true, as each is but a different stage in the journey, the aim of which is the perfect conception of the Vedas. Hence, too, we not only tolerate, but we Hindus accept every religion, praying in the mosque of the Mohammedans, worshipping before the fire of the Zoroastrians, and kneeling before the cross of the Christians, knowing that all the religions, from the lowest fetishism to the highest absolutism, mean so many attempts of the human soul to grasp and realise the infinite, each determined by the conditions of its birth and association, and each of them marking a stage of progress. We gather all these flowers and bind them with the twine of love, making a wonderful bouquet of worship.

If I am God, then my soul is a temple of the Highest, and my every motion should be a worship—love for love's sake, duty for duty's sake, without hope of reward or fear of punishment. Thus my religion means expansion, and expansion means realisation and perception in the highest sense—no mumbling words or genuflections. Man is to become divine, realising the divine more and more from day to day in an endless progress.[*]

(*Complete Works of Swami Vivekananda*, 1992, vol. 1, pp. 329–32.)

---

[*] Summary of a lecture delivered before the Ethical Society, Brooklyn, at the Pouch Gallery in Clinton Avenue, on the 30th December, 1894. Reproduced from the *Brooklyn Standard Union*.

BOOKS ON AND BY
SWAMI VIVEKANANDA

For a detailed Price List , please write to:

Advaita Ashrama
Publication Department
5 Dehi Entally Road
Calcutta 700 014